Cold
Theater

Twelvth
Night

349-T

Steve
Peters

Y0-CDR-974

NOAH
'932-2494

Third Edition

The NY Agent Book

K Callan

Third Edition—revised and updated

© K Callan 1993
ISBN 0-9617336-9-1
ISSN 1058-191X

First Edition 1987
Second Edition 1990
Third Edition 1993

Other books by K Callan
An Actor's Workbook
The LA Agent Book
The NY Agent Book
How to Sell Yourself as an Actor
The Life of the Party
The Script Is Finished — Now, What Do I Do?

Design: Devine Design, Burbank, California
Illustrations: Stephen Turk
Photography: Van Williams
Editing: Kristi Nolte

Thank you...

NY Agents for giving of your time, trust and insights to help me create this book.

Adele Weitz for helping me become computer literate and for continuing computer support.

Dedication

This book is dedicated to the memory of Oliver Hailey who encouraged me to write.

Introduction

You are talented, trained and your instrument is tuned and ready to play. The next step is finding an agent. Or is it?

This book deals with all aspects of actor/agent relationships at various stages of one's career. The first agent, the free-lance alliance, the exclusive relationship, confronting the agent with problems, salvaging the bond, and if need be, leaving the partnership.

There's information for the newcomer, help for the seasoned actor and encouragement for everybody.

My consciousness about the business has been raised dramatically a result of meeting and interviewing over 100 agents in New York and Los Angeles. The process was just like every other part of the business, sometimes scary, sometimes wonderful, sometimes painful, but always a challenge. Mostly, the agents were funny, interesting, dynamic, warm and not at all as unapproachable as they seem when you are on the outside looking in.

Just like a new appliance, you'll get more help from this book if you will follow the instructions: Read *straight through* and do not skip around. The first part provides background to assess the information in the latter part of the book.

Fight the urge to run to the agent listings and read about a particular agent. Until you absorb more information regarding evaluating agents, you're not in a position to make an intelligent choice.

If you read the agents' quotes with some perception, you will gain insights not only into their character, but into how the business is really run and you'll notice whose philosophy is comparable to yours. Taken by themselves the quotes might only be interesting, but considered in context and played against the insights of other agents, they are revealing and educational.

It's been a gratifying experience to come in contact with all the agents and all the actors I have met as a result of my books. Since, I'm asking the questions for all of us, let me know if I've missed something you deem important and I'll include it in my next book. Write to me c/o Sweden Press at the address on the back of the book.

K Callan
Los Angeles, California

Contents

Will Getting an Agent Change Your Life?

Whether you are an aspiring actor, writer, director or any other supplicant in show business, getting an agent takes on enormous significance in the quest for credibility in show business.

It seems you can't do business without an agent, and unless you are already making money, it's impossible to get an agent to talk to you, take a meeting or in any other way validate your existence.

Despite many obstacles, untried people still manage to enter the business hourly. These new people may be related to others in the business or otherwise connected giving them entre. Those without this benefit need to be driven, clever, ingenious and of course, very talented. Many are all of the above.

Show biz is a glamour business. Where else can you get heartbreak, pain, disappointment, and rejection, plus big time money, sex and fame all at the same time? In order to join the club and become a working writer, actor, director, producer (not even a star, you understand), you must have grit, drive, ingenuity, talent, professionalism, craft, patience, stability, wit, style, grace, faith and hope. Many get by without charity.

For all of you neither related nor connected, I've interviewed over 100 agents in Los Angeles and New York who represent actors for the theater, film, and television. I have asked them what they are looking for, how neophyte actors might get their attention and other related questions. My experience interviewing agents has led me to believe they are a charming and civilized lot.

Why do we have to have agents?

Agents exist because there is a need. The buyers could not possibly cull through all the actors who would be sitting on their doorways if there were not some kind of screening process.

Although it is possible to exist without an agent via an attorney, manager or one's own entrepreneurial skills, this book is about the pros and cons of having an agent, what an actor has a right to expect from an agent, what he doesn't have a right to expect, when it's time to look for an agent, how to attract an agent and how to have a rewarding synergistic relationship with the agent you choose.

What is an agent anyway?

The dictionary (which knows very little about show business) has many definitions for the word *agent*. By combining a couple I've come up with:

A force acting in place of another, effecting a certain result by driving, inciting, or setting in motion; a go between.

What does he do? Where do I find an agent? Do I need an agent? How can I get an agent to talk to me? What would I say to an agent? Are there rules of behavior? How can I tell if an agent is a good agent? When is the right time to look for an agent? What if they all want to sign me, how can I choose the right agent? What if no an agent wants to sign me, do I have to go back to Iowa? What will I tell my family?

Tell your family that you are taking classes, making the rounds and being an actor. When you get an agent you will let them know, but that whether or not you have an agent has nothing to do with the fact that you are pursuing your dream. Being an actor is not about being employed. Being an actor is about looking for work. Tell them this is making you happy and that making money will only be icing on the cake. Civilians (those who have never pursued a job in show business) and would-be actors who are still in school, can't possibly empathize. They have no idea what any artist goes through in pursuit of employment and/or an agent. They're not going to understand anything except your name up on the screen in big letters saying: *Starring*.

What does an agent do?

Actors frequently ask exactly what it is that an agent does. In the most basic function, the agent, acting on your behalf, sets in motion a series of events that result in your having a shot at a job. He gets you in the door for meetings, interviews and auditions. He calls up his contacts and persuades them to give you an audition over all the other hundreds of actors who want to be seen for a particular job.

In addition, he makes phone calls, sends out your picture, talks about you incessantly, builds you up, encourages you, tells you to get a haircut, a shrink, a mate, a job, a life. Many things he does for you, you may never know about: There's not always a direct correlation between a phone call and a job. The road is more interesting than that.

Do I need one?

Most actors possesses neither the contacts, information, nor appetite for representing themselves over the long haul. It

most instances, however, it is necessary to be your own
first agent; finding your own first job(s), getting to know
casting directors, sending out flyers about your work,
reading casting notices and going to open auditions. Once
you have a body of work and have the option of concentrating on your acting and having someone else shoulder the
major portion of keeping you visible, you will undoubtedly
want an agent's help with your career.

How can I get an agent to talk to me?

It seems a simple enough task, really. After all, you have
spent years studying, perfecting your instrument; dancing
class, singing lessons, working on your craft, examing your
persona and building a resume that denotes credibility.

Haven't you?

How can I tell if someone is a good agent?

The agent I would want has been spending his time getting
to know the business, seeing every play, television show,
and film, watching the development of actors, writers,
directors, and producers, meeting people on all levels of the
business, networking, staying visible, and communicating.

He's met casting directors and developed relationships with
them. He only represents those actors whose work he
personally knows so that when he tells a casting director an
actor is perfect for the role and has the background for it,
the casting director trusts his word.

That's the way the agent builds *his* credibility; it doesn't
happen any faster than the actor building his resume.

Besides getting the actor the appropriate audition, the agent
has to be prepared to negotiate a brilliant contract when the
actor wins the job. That entails knowing all the contracts,

rules, and regulations of the Screen Actors Guild, Actors Equity and American Federation of Radio and Television Artists, as well as having an understanding of the marketplace and knowing what others at similar career levels are getting for similar jobs.

He must then have the courage, style, and judgment to stand up to the buyers in asking what is fair for the actor without giving in to the temptation to sell the actor down the river financially in favor of his future relationship with the producers or casting directors or without becoming too grandiose and turning everyone off.

And that's not all:

• *I think the agent's real job is to be with a client when they're down. It's very easy to be on someone's side when they're making a lot of money and they're very successful. It's not always that easy to be on their side when they don't have work, and they don't know what they're doing and they're depressed and they feel insecure.*

Ellen Curren
The Gersh Agency New York

• *I feel that I'm responsible for my clients' attitudes and for their self-confidence.*

Kenneth Kaplan
Innovative Artists

• *If we have a client that we haven't talked to in two weeks, we sit down and call them. It's also important for him to call and say,* I haven't talked to you in two weeks. I just wanted to plug in. How is everything? *That's the way to be a client. You've gotta have your input. If you just sit back and wait for it to happen, it's not going to happen. It's just not.*

Ellen Curren
The Gersh Agency New York

• *What is typical of most agencies is not typical here. Our clients wander in to see us and we make the time. We service them. They pay our bills. Our commodity is not the producer. Our commodity is the actor.*

Louis J. Ambrosio
Ambrosio/Mortimer

• *If you sign someone, if you agree to be their agent, no matter how big the agency gets, you've agreed to be there for them and that's your responsibility.*

Kenneth Kaplan
Innovative Artists

• *I have tried, with as much speed as possible to let clients know that this is really an alliance that's built and that it's very much a commitment, that eventually they can truly feel comfortable not seeking the approval of their agent. I think the confidence factor is so important to an actor. They are at the mercy of so many people. The kind of relationship you have with your client, if they can sense a comfortability factor, a compatibility factor, it builds, so that communication comes along with real trust. And then you really work in tandem with each other. It becomes a mutuality.*

Peter Strain
Peter Strain & Associates

Although it might be nice to be pals with your agent, it is not necessary. One of the best agents I ever had was never available to me to help me feel good when all was dark.

He did, however, initiate new business for me, negotiate well, have impeccable taste, was well regarded in the community and had access to everyone in the business. He also believed in me, did not lose faith when I did not win every audition, gave me good *notes* on my performances, clued me into mistakes I was making, and made a point of viewing my work at every opportunity. Oh yes, and he returned my phone calls.

Franchised Agents

Besides being trained, compatible, credible, committed and able to communicate, you will want to have an agent who is *franchised*. To be a franchised agent, the agency must have a license to operate from the state, agree to abide by the Agency Rules and Regulations of the Screen Actors Guild or any of the performer unions involved and have some experience as an agent.

An actor who is a member of SAG or one of the other performers unions must be represented by a franchised agent. He can represent himself anytime he wants, but if an agent conducts business for him, the agent must have signed an agreement with one of the guilds. That agreement is called a *franchise*.

Just because an agent is franchised is no guarantee that the he/she is ethical, knowledgeable and/or effective. Since he is franchised, he probably is, but this is such an important decision, be wise and check him out.

Wrap Up

Agent
✓   a force acting in place of another, effecting a certain result by driving, inciting, or setting in motion, a go between.

Agent's Job
✓   to become *connected* to the buyers
✓   to get the actor meetings, interviews and auditions
✓   to negotiate salary and billing
✓   to have credibility, taste and courage

**Welcome to the
Big Apple**

I asked a lot of agents what they felt was the first thing an actor should do when he first *got off the bus* in either Los Angeles or New York and a couple laughed and said, *Get back on.* They were joking, but it's not bad advice.

Coming into a new environment (no matter how long you have waited to get there) requires a period of adjustment. Don't add the stress of agent-hunting until you have an apartment and are *ready* to be seen. First impressions are always the strongest, make sure yours is a good one. As J. Michael Bloom puts it: *You're only new once.*

• *Get a job. Keep yourself in a good state all the time. You can't be broke. It does not work. Secure yourself a job in whatever it is that you can do, whether it be as a waiter or as a secretary, where they give you leniency to go out on auditions. Being a starving actor does not work. What works is to be healthy and to keep some money in your pocket so that you are not hysterical while you are doing this. I don't come from the point of view that you have to suffer to be an actor.*
> Bruce Levy
> Bruce Levy Agency

• *Before an actor begins to look for an agent, he should establish a secure foundation. He or she needs a place to live and/or a job and some friends to talk to and pictures or* at least a facsimile of pictures. *It's very important that they have a comfortable place to go to during the day and be settled so they don't carry that into an agent's or a manager's office. It's not helpful or necessary. They think an agent or a manager will turn into a surrogate mother/father/teacher/confessor and that really isn't their role. Actors do that and then get disappointed when they aren't taken care of right away. I think it's better to come in as a fully secure person so you can be sold that way. Otherwise, too much development time is wasted.*

Gary Krasny
The Krasny Office, Inc.

• *You want to come to New York with training and with a base because when you meet people, the way you are at that moment is how they're going to remember you. If you meet people and you're not at your best, that's going to be the way they remember you.*

It's all those silly things your mother told you when you were growing up and you hated and they were right all along. It's really is how you are the first day of class. That's how the teachers always remember you. Sometimes you can shift that image, but it's hard.

Flo Rothaker
DGRW

• *Unless you're 17 and gorgeous, it's a waste of time to make rounds. Ringing doorbells, slipping pictures under doors, sending pictures. We probably get about 15 pictures a day - that's how we get our cardboard.*

Unless Shirley Rich or someone recommends you, it's pretty impossible. I think they should knock themselves out trying to get a valid showcase. Lord knows that's hard, but it can't be any harder than ringing doorbells trying to get a good agent.

Monty Silver
Silver, Kass
& Massetti/East

• *There's no simple straight line answer. I think the philosophical basis is to find a way to work as much as possible, because the more you get your work out there, the more people have an opportunity to respond to it. Everyone in this business who is not an actor makes their living by recognizing talented actors.*

The smartest thing a young playwright can do is to know, to spot, a good young talented actor so that when they do the showcase of the play he can recommend the actor. That's going to make his play look better.

There are a number of stage directors in New York who all they can really do (to be candid) is read a script and cast well and then stay out of the way. That can often be all you need. So that's the point; casting directors, agents, playwrights, directors, even stage managers are going to remember good actors. If they want to get ahead in their business, the more they remember good actors, the better off they're gonna be. Having your work out there is the crucial thing.

Studying is important because it keeps you ready. Nobody is going to give you six weeks to get your instrument ready. It's, Here's the audition; do it now, *so I believe in showcases. Actors tend to be too linear in their thinking. They think,* Okay. I did this showcase and no agent came and nobody asked me to come to their office so it was a complete waste of time.

Well, I don't believe that. First of all, even a bad production is going to teach a young actor a lot of important things. Second of all, generally if you do a good job in a play, it produces another job. Often it's in another showcase. Often, it's a year later, so if you're looking for direct links, you never see them.

What tends to happen is somebody calls you up and says, I saw you in that show and you were really terrific and would you like to come do this show? *It's like out of the blue, and it can take a long time. You may have to do eight great showcases or readings or anything, but if your work is out there, there is an opportunity for people to get* excited and if it isn't out there, then that opportunity doesn't exist.

It doesn't matter how terrific you are in the office and how charming you are. None of that matters.

Tim Angle
Don Buchwald & Ass.

• *I would go to class. I would do anything I could. I would not sit around feeling sorry for myself. If I couldn't get someone to hire me as an actor, I'd get a group of my friends in the same position; I'd move all the furniture to one side and I'd do a play in my living room and then call the agents and ask them to come see me.*

Lionel Larner
Lionel Larner

Actually, that's what Carol Burnett did when she first came to New York. If you want to read a really great book about making it in show business, read her autobiography, One More Time, (Random House, 1986); it's inspiring.

• *I'm assuming that someone getting off the bus in New York has been trained and that theater is his goal. He or she should try to get affiliated with one of the theater companies like Circle Rep or Ensemble Studio Theater or Manhattan Class Company. He or she should volunteer his services in any capacity at any of those places.*

Also try to get into class because of the information that comes from that and other actors available to you. A whole network can be created from that. If you are in some kind of venue where there's a possibility, even in a class, of inviting someone to come see something, at least that gives you a step up making some contacts in terms of getting an agent.

Brian Riordan
J. Michael Bloom

If you are a crazy person in general, you really must get your life together before even thinking about show business. This business takes people and chews them up and spits them out for breakfast unless they remain extremely focused and provide another life for themselves.

• *There are some people I know who are brilliant actors, but I'm not willing to take responsibility for their careers because I know the rest of their life is not in order.*
Flo Rothaker
DGRW

If your life *is* in order, find a support group to help you keep it that way before you enter the fray.

Build a Support Group

Life is easier with friends. Begin to build relationships with your peers. There are those who say to build friendships with people who already have what you want and I understand the thinking, but it's not my idea of a good time.

It's a lot easier to live on a shoestring and/or deal with constant rejection if your friends are going through the same thing. If your friend is starring on a television show or is king of commercials and has plenty of money while you are scrambling to pay the rent, it is going to be harder to keep perspective about where you are in the process. It takes different people differing amounts of time to make the journey. Having friends who understand that will make it easier for all of you.

Be positive. It's one of the most important things you can do for yourself. Ruth Gordon's perspective is instructive:

• *Life is getting through the moment. The philosopher William James says to cultivate the cheerful attitude. Now nobody had more trouble than he did — except me. I had more trouble in my life than anybody. But your first big trouble can be a bonanza if you live through it. Get through the first trouble, you'll probably make it through the next one.*

"The Careerist Guide
to Survival"
Paul Rosenfield
The Los Angeles Times
April 25, 1982

If you don't know enough people to start your own group, explore one of the 12-Step Groups. There's comfort for every problem from Alcoholics Anonymous to the *other* AA: Artists Anonymous. Even though this group is for all kinds of artists, you'll find a majority are actors and writers. There is also ACA (Adult Children of Alcoholics), NA (Narcotics Anonymous), OA (Overeaters Anonymous), etc.

No matter who you are, there is a group for you to identify with that will provide you with confidential support for free. You'll be better served if you don't look to these groups for your social life. They supply a forum to talk about what is bothering you, but support groups are not your family and though helpful, they're not your best friends, either. Put energy into your personal relationships to fill those needs. You create your life. Will Rogers said, *People are about as happy as they want to be.* I agree, I believe we all get what we really want.

If you are a member of a performers union (SAG, AEA, AFTRA), check for support groups within the union or get involved in one of their committees. You'll have the chance to be involved in a productive activity with your peers on a regular basis that will give you a family and a focus.

If you are in an impossible relationship or if you have any kind of addiction problem, the business is only going to intensify the problems. Deal with these things first.

Showcases

Try to get into a showcase. The process of auditioning for showcases is valid and a good experience in itself.

• *I think they should try to find a showcase which presents them in a castable light, in a role that's appropriate and that is convenient for agents to get to. You can't get me to go to Brooklyn.*

Before they invite agents, they should be very careful (and perhaps have professional advice) as to whether or not this is a worthwhile thing to invite agents to. You can sometimes engender more hostility wasting an agent's evening if it's abominable.

Phil Adelman
The Gage Group

• *Actors have to be selective about the kind of showcases they get involved in. A lot of times an actor has always wanted to play "The Cherry Orchard" so they'll do a showcase down in a small basement on the Lower East Side, but the fact is that people in the business are really not interested in going to see that.*

Your expectations should be lower. You're not going to get an agent as a result of that, but your director may direct something else or you may meet somebody, or another person in the cast may say, There's another showcase over here. *It's a network.*

Joanna Ross
William Morris Agency

When you find yourself encountering agents in social situations, learn to read what is going on. An agent may be interested in you, but it's like dating; he wants a sign to know it's okay to proceed. Be alert to similar messages from him.

• *I'm not the kind of agent that's going to go up to you and say,* Who's your agent? I'm better than he is. *We're in a highly competitive business. It's bad enough already. I don't have to make it worse. I don't like people to steal my clients, so I don't steal others.*

> Pat House
> The Actors Group

• *Would you expect a lawyer you meet at a party to say* Who's your lawyer? *But you expect me as an agent to say,* Who's your agent? *I'm a professional. You hire me to do a job. I can either accept it or not. I'm not soliciting work. I get other people jobs, not myself.*

> Barry Douglas
> DGRW

Be alert and aware for signs of interest from anyone; directors, producers, etc., and follow up on it. Ask if there is anything you can do to help with a current project.

• *When you finally get your meeting with the agent, you can't sit there and tremble and be intimidated, that's your time to impress.*

> Lionel Larner
> Lionel Larner

Get a Place to Live

Even though it's New York, the problem is not unsolvable. If you are a union member, check out the bulletin board for sublet information as well as the bulletin board at The Drama Book Store. Theatrical answering services know everything that is going on in town (Why not? They hear all your messages.) For that reason, they are a good source of information. They offer their bulletin boards to subscribers to list sublets, furniture for sale, etc. The show business newspapers <u>Backstage</u> and <u>Showbusiness</u> offer even more ways to plug into the grapevine.

There are actor-friendly neighborhoods in the City: West Beth is an artistic community in the West Village with subsidized housing and a long waiting list, but sublets are available since actors are always going out of town for jobs and The Manhattan Plaza which is in midtown on the West Side. Both of these artist havens offer classes and are plugged into the creative forces of the city.

Areas in which rents are cheaper are the Lower East Side, below Wall Street, Chinatown, and some areas of what used to be called Hell's Kitchen in the far West 40s.

Some churches and YMCA/YWCAs have a limited amount of relatively inexpensive housing available on a temporary basis. There is also a new Youth Hostel in New York. For information consult New York Convention and Visitors Bureau, Two Columbus Circle, New York, 10019.

There are those fabled $75 per month apartments that keep us all salivating but they have been occupied for 100s of years by the same tenant. Don't allow yourself to keep from finding suitable housing because you are waiting for one of those *fabulous deals*. You don't want to use up all your *good luck* getting a swell apartment for 35¢. Save your luck for your *big break* and you can afford to pay full price.

More and more people are finding housing in Brooklyn, Queens, New Jersey or Staten Island. When I first arrived in New York, I briefly considered New Jersey (particularly because I had children), but after a lot of soul searching, I realized that my dream was to come to *New York City*. If I was going to starve, let it be while living my dream all the way. Not everyone's dream is so particularized. There are hundreds of actors who live out of the city successfully and prefer it.

Getting to Know the City

It's easy to get around the Island of Manhattan. If you are not directionally inclined, this is your chance to understand about north, south, east, and west. The Hudson River is west and guess where the East River is?

You'll notice as you travel uptown (north) that the numbers get larger and as you go downtown toward Wall Street, Chinatown, and the Statue of Liberty (south) that the numbers get smaller. The numbers stop at Houston (pronounced how-ston). Then you have to deal with names, so you will have to learn a few names.

The quickest way to get anywhere is on a bicycle if you have the courage, but that's too scary for me, so I walk. Cabs are expensive and frequently very slow. Fastest transportation is the subway. Many people don't like to use it, but I've personally never had any trouble. Go to any subway station for a free map. There is also a map in every New York City phone book. You'll find lists and addresses of New York Theaters in the same place.

There are subways that only go up and down the East Side (Lexington Avenue) and some that only go up and down the West Side (Seventh Avenue) and some (the E & F) that do both. There are some that only go crosstown, at 14th Street, 42nd Street and 59th Street. Buses are great for shorter hops, but you must have exact change or a subway token. It makes sense to buy a supply of tokens so you don't have to stand in line each time. You can buy tokens at banks as well as the subway stations. Some stations don't have manned token booths at all times, so keep a supply in your pocket.

I can walk across town in about 20 minutes; you probably can, too. There used to be a great guide available that some enterprising chap (an actor, of course) published that listed all the ways to get around town without going outdoors, using subway tunnels, connecting buildings, etc.

Crosstown blocks (they go east and west) are about three times as long as downtown blocks (which go north and south). It takes about the same amount of time to walk from 42nd to 59th Streets as it takes to go from Lexington Avenue to Broadway.

I've included a map to give you an overview; the Broadway theater district, the Public Theater, the Statue of Liberty, The Theater Library at Lincoln Center, the TKTS Booth (half price tickets to Broadway and Off-Broadway shows), the various networks, bookstores, etc.

In the front of the phone book you'll find a guide to figuring out cross streets to numbered addresses. For instance, if you are at 1501 Broadway, you are between 43rd and 44th Streets. Tear the guide out and put it in the front of your appointment book, it will save you time and shoe leather.

In the meantime, here's the map and it's index.

1. ABC Television at 54th Street
    1330 Avenue of the Americas

2. Actors Equity Association (AEA)
    165 West 46th Street
    East of Broadway

3. Actor's Studio
    432 West 44th Street
    Between 9th & 10th Avenues

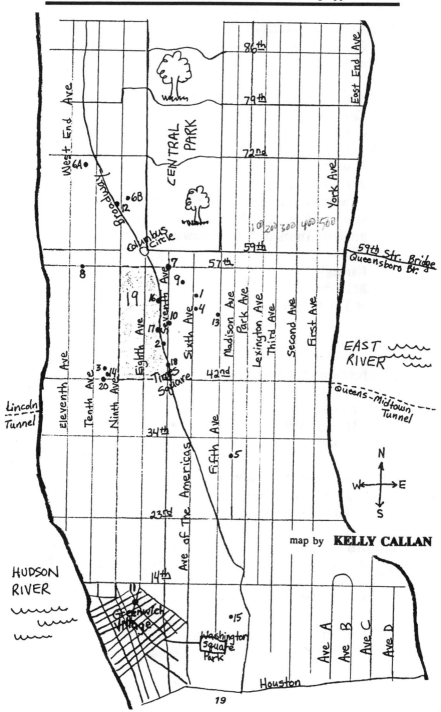

map by **KELLY CALLAN**

4. American Federation of Radio & Television Artists
    260 Madison Avenue
    at 38th Street

5. American Academy of Dramatic Arts
    120 Madison Avenue
    at 32nd Street

6. Applause Theater Books
    211 West 71st Street
    between Broadway & West End Avenue
    also at 100 West 67th Street
    between Amsterdam & Broadway

7. Carnegie Hall
    881 7th Avenue
    at 57th Street

8. CBS Television Studios
    524 West 57th Street
    between 10th & 11th Avenues

9. City Center
    131 West 55th Street
    between 6th & 7th Avenues

10. The Drama Book Shop
    723 Seventh Avenue
    at 48th Street, 2nd Floor

11. HB Studios
    20 Bank Street
    in the Village
    West of 8th Avenue

12. Lincoln Center/Theater Library
    144 West 66th Street
    at Broadway

13. NBC Television
    30 Rockefeller Plaza
    5th Avenue & 49th Street

14. Manhattan Plaza
    the block bounded by 42nd and 43rd Streets
    and 8th & 9th Avenues

15. The Public Theater
    425 Lafayette Street
    South of 14th Street, East of Fifth Avenue

16. Screen Actors Guild
    1700 Broadway
    at 53rd Street

17. TKTS (Half Price Theater Tickets)
    North End of Times Square

18. Theater District (Broadway)
    42nd to 57th Streets
    Broadway to 9th Avenue

19. Theater Row
    42nd Street
    between 9th & 10th Avenues

Get a Job

Once you have found a place to live, it is important for more than financial reasons to find a job.

• *If I were an actor just in from the boondocks without any experience whatsoever, I think I would get myself hired somewhere in a theater; I mean doing anything, selling programs or candy or watching the phone, or the stage door. I would get myself a job in the business because you learn a tremendous amount. I also think it shows the determination because you're not looking immediately for the reward before doing the work. We all have to pay our dues.*

Lionel Larner
Lionel Larner

Having a job gives form to your life. It gives you a place to go every day, a family of people to relate to and helps you feel a part of the city much more quickly. Nothing feeds depression more than sitting at home alone in a strange city. Even if you know the city, you'll find as time goes on, that activity is the friend of the actor. Depression feeds on itself and must not be allowed to get out of hand.

If you are fortunate and tenacious enough to find a job in the business, you'll find you're being paid to continue your education. There is no way in the world you can learn what it's like to be in the business without being in the business. Not only that, you have a place to go to everyday with the people you want to be with, who are interested in the same things that you are.

• *Always be available. Don't say you are an actor if you have a 9-5 job. If you must waitress, do it at night.*

Sharon Carry
The Carry Company

Even more important than a job with contacts is a job with flexible working hours. If you can combine the two, that's the best. You will learn who is having auditions, how people go about getting *up* for them, who other actors think are good teachers and a wealth of other information. As soon as you are working in the business in any category, you are *in the system* and on your way. I don't want to imply that coming up with one of these jobs is the easiest task in the world, but it is definitely worth the effort.

Get into an Acting Class

When you first arrive in town, it is difficult to know right away who is a good teacher and who isn't. It's hard to know whether or not a person is even *trying* to be a good teacher or is just there to take your money so be wise and investigate. One of my favorite agents, the late Michael Kingman made a good point about acting teachers:

• *No one can teach you to act; a teacher can only stimulate your imagination. You must find the one who does that for you.*

> Michael Kingman
> Michael Kingman Agency

And learning to act is just one of the important reasons to get into a really good class:

• *The best way to get some resources is to take some kind of class, to get to know other actors. I think your most valuable information comes from working actors. If working actors are already working, who is their agent? Why are they working? Where did they go to school? What have they done? It's your best resource.*

> Ellen Curren
> Gersh Agency New York

• *I recommend that people shop around a bit. A teacher that I might like might not suit that person's personality or they might have already fulfilled those needs and need to move on to something different. There are specific classes; people that give audition classes, others give tape audition classes. If there is a weakness in a particular actor, then you can focus on that specifically.*

> Brian Riordan
> J. Michael Bloom

• *Training is very important. To put oneself in visible projects in the city. To network themselves and to have a realistic view of themselves, too.*

Louis Ambrosio
Ambrosio/Mortimer

• *Audit classes. See the atmosphere of the class. If it seems to be an environment to stimulate healthy growth in you, then check out the technique. Technique is only part of it. First, you want to be sure that you are going to be in a creative space, then you find out about the technique. Is this the place where I can expand? Is this a place where I can fall on my face where they will support me in picking myself up?*

Bruce Levy
Bruce Levy Agency

• *Like anything else that you're going to invest money and time in, an actor should shop around and see what's best for him. See someone whose work you admire and find out who they study with and audit that class.*

Jerry Kahn
Jerry Kahn, Inc.

• *Choose an acting class that keeps expanding you, not only your acting abilities, but your creativity and your being. You need constant expansion. If you are not getting that or if you feel closed down in a class, do not continue. If you feel closed down in class, that's happening to your auditions, also.*

Bruce Levy
Bruce Levy Agency

Teachers

Here is a list of well-regarded teachers in New York. Some I know personally, some are recommendations of several agents I respect or of other actors whose judgment I trust. Some are more expensive than others. If I have mentioned an institution like The Actors Studio or HB, know that all teachers there are not equal. You'll need to get a list of who is there and hang out at the place a little to see who the students are. The coolest students will usually be in the best classes. Audit classes to see who seems most right to you. See at least three so that you can compare.

Actor's Studio	Bob McAndrew
American Academy of	Bob Modica
Dramatic Arts	Larry Moss
Paul Austin	Leonard Peters
William Esper	Suzanne Ringrose (soaps)
Aaron Frankel	Sam Schacht
Kathryn Gateley	Jacqueline Segal
HB Studio	Joan See (commercials)
Uta Hagen	Terry Shreiber
Wynn Handman	Alice Spivak
Bill Hickey	Steve Strimpel
Barbara Hipkiss	Kate McGregor Stuart
Michael Howard	Janet Ward (at Strasberg's)
Peter Kass	Bill Woodman (auditions)

• *I have a pet theory that* studying *is going to come back amongst people who are actually working professionally all the time. I hear a lot of our clients who are working continually talking about their desire to get back to class.*
> Joanna Ross
> William Morris Agency

In a good class, you will begin to meet other actors and become more knowledgeable about the marketplace.

Before you come to New York

If you are reading this book as a student preparing to study, consider one of the important theater schools if you can afford it and if they accept you. It does make a difference, not only are some schools significantly superior to others, but there is a group of schools that is universally accepted as the most comprehensive training for young actors and whose cachet instantly alerts the antennae of employers.

Originally a collective of Schools of Professional Training for Actors referred to as *The Leagues,* these schools offered rigorous conservatory training. The official collective no longer exists, but those schools still offer graduates who are immediately thought by buyers (casting directors, agents, producers, directors, etc.) to be the *creme de la creme* of new young actors, surely where the next Meryl Streep and Paul Newman are coming from (and did).

If you graduate from one of the prestigious theater schools, you are definitely ahead of the game as far as agents in NY/LA are concerned. And in fact, you probably *will* be better trained. Actors in these programs are routinely scouted by agents and sometimes procure representation as early as their freshman year.

Prestigious Theater Schools

* formerly in the Leagues collective.

*

American Conservatory Theater
Edward Hastings
450 Geary Street
San Francisco, CA 94102
(415) 749-2200

American Repertory Theater
Robert Brustein, Artistic Director
Harvard University
Byerly Hall, 8 Garden Street
Cambridge, Massachusetts 02138
(617) 495-2668

* **Boston University**
Robert Morgan
121 Bay State Road
Boston, Massachusetts 02215
(617) 353-2300

* **Carnegie Mellon**
Elisabeth Orion
5000 Forbes Avenue
Pittsburgh, Pennsylvania 15213
(412) 268-2082

Catholic University
William H. Graham, Chairperson
620 Michigan Ave. NE
Washington, District of Columbia 20064
(202) 319-5358

* **Juilliard School**
Michael Langham
Lincoln Center
New York City, New York 10023
(212) 799-5000

* **New York University**
Arthur Barstow, Chairperson
25 West 4th Street
New York City, New York 10012
(212) 998-1212

* **North Carolina School of the Arts**
Robert Francesconi
200 Waughtown Street
Winston-Salem, North Carolina 27717-2189
(919) 770-3399

* **Southern Methodist University**
Dean Charlie Helfert
P. O. Box 286
Dallas, Texas 75275
(214) 692-3217

* **State University of New York (at Purchase)**
Israel Hicks
735 Anderson Hill Road
Purchase, New York 10577
(914) 251-6000

* **University of California (at San Diego)**
Adele Shank, Chairperson
101 Administration Bldg. 2nd floor
La Jolla, California 92093
(619) 534-6889

* **Yale Drama School**
Yale University
Dean Lloyd Richards
P. O. Box 1302 A
Yale Station
New Haven, Connecticut 06520
(203) 432-1505

All of these schools offer excellent training, but they are hard to get into and very expensive, so be wise and investigate more than one. This type of education requires a big commitment of time and money. Consider carefully in order to choose the school that is right for you.

Even if you are educated at the best schools and come to New York highly touted with interest from agents, there will still be a period of adjustment:

• *When you come out of school, you gotta freak out for a while. And there's just not anything else that can be done*

*about it because (particularly actors who were in very high
powered training programs) they've been working night and
day doing seven different things at once and now they're
suddenly out and dry and nothing. It takes a year at least,
to kind of get over that and learn to be unemployed. And
they have to learn to deal with that. It happens to
everybody. It's not just you.*

Joanna Ross
William Morris Agency

Assess the Marketplace

Analyzing the marketplace and using that information
wisely can save you years of unfocused activity. If you
were starting any other kind of business, you would
certainly expect to do extensive research to see if there
really was a need for the product you had decided to sell.

Besides looking at actors and noting who is working, notice
and keep a file on casting directors, producers, directors,
and writers. Note which writers seem to be writing parts
for people like you. Become an intelligent entrepreneur.

Learn and practice remembering the names of *everybody*.
Know who the critics are. Note those whose taste agrees
with yours. Think of this educational process as your
Ph.D. If you are going to be a *force* in the business, begin
now to think of yourself as such and assume your rightful
place.

*a force: energy, power, strength, vigor, vitality, impact,
value, weight.*

With each new detail about the business that you ingest and
have ready at your fingertips, your vitality increases. With
each play you read, see, rehearse, perform in, with each
writer, actor, director, casting director, costumer, etc., that
you support, your weight increases.

• *I feel sorry for the people who spend all their time trying to use various forms of manipulation to get an agent while their contemporaries are working and learning. And the ones working at working will rise right up. The people who were assuming it's some kind of game will disappear.*

> Fifi Oscard
> Fifi Oscard Agency, Inc.

Emergencies

If you are a member of any of the performing unions (SAG, AEA or AFTRA) these unions all have some kind of financial assistance available to members in an emergency situation. If you are not a member of a union, talk to your acting teacher and ask for advice.

There are also many city agencies equipped to deal with people in need. There is low-cost counseling available. Call universities for information. Also look in the front of the white pages of the phone book for city agencies.

Invaluable Publications

Ross Reports Television is a monthly that prints names and addresses of agents, casting directors, networks, unions, advertising agencies as well as other helpful information. It's not necessary to buy it monthly, changes don't happen *that* often, but if you are not in regular touch with a specific group of agents, get a new copy every three months or so. Sold at The Drama Book Store plus most good newsstands and available directly from the publisher:

Television Index, Inc.
40-29 27th St.,
Long Island City, NY 11101.
Phone 718-937-3990.

Backstage and ShowBusiness are weekly showbiz newspapers listing theater, film, and television information of every kind. Available at most newsstands.

We are all embarked on an exciting adventure. Some of us are further down the road than others. It's important to enjoy the journey. From the perspective of time, I look at my life and realize that the times of great struggle were frequently the most rewarding.

When we are employed, we feel as though we will never be *un*employed again. We will. When we are not working we feel as though we will never work again. We will. What goes up must come down and vice versa. Learn to explore the ride. It's fascinating.

Wrap Up

Personal
- ✓ support group
- ✓ family
- ✓ teachers

Geographical
- ✓ phone books
- ✓ maps
- ✓ NY Convention Bureau

Professional
- ✓ job in business
- ✓ acting class/teachers
- ✓ theatrical publications

Changing Agents

Don't skip this chapter just because you don't yet have an agent. One of the best ways to learn what you want in an agent it to discern what you don't want. Discussing problems others are having with their agents gives insight into cause, effect and how to make the most of your relationship once you have one.

• *Jumping ship every six months (which a lot of actors do) only serves to hurt the actor because everybody knows about it and it shows that the actor can't necessarily get a job because something's wrong and it's not because of the agent.*

> Gary Krasny
> The Krasny Office

The temptation is to leave your agent if you are not working. There may be many reasons why you aren't working that have nothing to do with your agent:

⊗   You might have gained or lost too much weight and now no one knows what to do with you.

⊗   You may be traveling into a new age category and have not yet finished the journey.

⊗   You might be getting stale and need to study. You might be having personal problems at home

that are reflected in your work; after all it's the
life energy that fuels our talent and craft.

⊗   The business might have changed, beautiful
      people may be in (or out).

How many projects can you list that had parts for you on
which you were not seen? And were there really parts for
you? You have to be right for a part not only physically
and temperamentally but also on an appropriate career level
as well.

•   *Actors don't do their homework. What part would you
have been sent up for on a Broadway show? Yes, it would
have been nice if you instead of Brad Pitt played the part in
that film, but no agent would have sent you for the part.*
                              Bret Adams
                              Bret Adams

Maybe the reason you want to change agents is that your
friend seems to be getting more auditions than you. It *is*
hard to listen to others talk about their good fortune when
you are home contemplating suicide, but before you get out
the razor blades, consider,

a.   You and your friend are not the same even
      though you may frequently be seen for the same
      roles.
b.   Some actors in their own depression, have been
      known to embroider the truth.
c.   Undoubtedly, you have gone on auditions when
      your friend did not.
d.   You may be on different career levels.

It may just not be *your turn* right now, but yours will come
eventually.

Perhaps your agent has not been treating you respectfully. Maybe he has been dishonest with you. Obviously if there have been financial improprieties, that's a good reason to leave.

There are other kinds of dishonesty; I know an actor who left his agent because the agent frequently told the actor how hard he had worked to get the actor in on projects on which the actor later found he had been requested.

Is your agent doing his part?

How can you tell if it's just not your turn or if the agent is off playing the horses? You can check with casting director friends, writers, directors and anyone else you know in the business. If you are being as involved as you should be, you'll be abreast of current projects so that you will have a realistic idea concerning projects for someone *like you*. Drop by the office with new pictures and see what is going on. Check with friends you trust to see if they have had any activity. Let them know you are not *fishing for information*, but just checking on your own paranoia, *Is my agent just not sending me out right now or is nothing going on*?

Another valid reason for leaving is if you feel you can't communicate with your agent.

• *The biggest problem in the actor/agent relationship is lack of communication.*

> Martin Gage
> The Gage Group

• *If the agent screws up a job, I think you should leave. If you don't get any appointments and you think you should be getting appointments, then you should move on to someone who is excited. If the agent doesn't take your phone calls, that's really a sign that there is something wrong. Sometimes you just have to get a fresh outlook. It works both ways.*

Gary Krasny
The Krasny Office

• *If an agent makes them feel uncomfortable when they call in, then they're at the wrong place.*

Ellen Curren
The Gersh Agency

But, communication works both ways.

• *I've heard actors say,* I haven't spoken to my agent in three months! *I've never heard an actor say,* I tried to get my agent on the phone for three months and I can't get through to him.

Bret Adams
Bret Adams

Maybe you are not getting the kinds of auditions you want.

• *It doesn't make any difference whether I send you on one thing or twelve things. You may like the feeling of activity. To me, that's baloney activity — motion. To me, it's being able to be sent on the right thing. The good thing. And being able to get the job.*

Marvin Starkman
Starkman Agency

• *Invariably an actor comes to me this happens to every agent and says,* I was with Jeff Hunter *or fill in the blank,* and he never got me up for movies. *When an actor says that to me and they are coming from an office that has a very good reputation, my response always is,* Have you said to yourself, am I meant for that? *Not everybody is going to make a movie. Not everybody is going to get a soap. Not everybody is going to get a Broadway show. The idea of,* I'm going to get it all, *is a laudable ambition but it always has to be tempered with (aside from the enormous break that sometimes comes to some people) is* this what I'm right for?

Alan Willig
Select Artists

• *I think you know what you've been submitted for. How many appointments you've gotten. You know the explanations of whatever. You have to take the explanation of the agent and weigh it.*

Jeff Hunter
William Morris Agency

Maybe you and your agent have different ideas regarding your potential. This is something that should have been ironed out before the contract was signed. Sometimes that conversation comes later in the relationship and it can be painful.

• *We have to tell actors what we think they can realistically expect. That pierces their dreams sometimes and they move on.*

Jeff Hunter
William Morris Agency

Many actors leave their agents because their careers have changed and they feel they can be better serviced with agents with different sets of contacts:

• *Every agent has different contacts. I may have fabulous theater contacts and absolutely no film contacts. I might bullshit and tell the actor I have film contacts, but if you were that actor and I didn't get you a film audition for a year, you'd be getting the sense that what I was telling you is not true.*

Beverly Anderson
Beverly Anderson

Perhaps you want to change agents because your level of achievement in the business has risen. You have now, through diligent work and study and possibly a lucky break, become an actor of greater stature than your agent. This is very possible if fortune has just smiled on you.

It can happen the other way, too, of course. One minute you're *hot* and the next moment you're not. You didn't necessarily do anything special to get yourself un-*hot* (frequently getting *hot* works the same way) but, unfortunately, when you're not *hot* at the big agencies, it might be difficult for you to get your agent on the phone. The larger agencies are not in the business to handle less-profitable jobs, so they either drop you or their lack of interest finally tells you that you're no longer on their level. This is the moment when you might be sorry you left that swell agent who worked so hard to get you started and engineered the big break for you. Will he want to see you now? He might. He might not. It depends on how you handled it when you left.

Maybe your career is doing okay but you feel you haven't progressed in several years.

Some actors leave their agents on a manager's advice. Sometimes that's a good idea, although it's possible the manager is just jealous of the long relationship the actor has with the agent and wants to put himself in the most powerful position with the actor.

Be realistic. If you have had a rewarding relationship with an agent over a long period of time, why have you taken on a manager, anyway? If you are just looking for a way to leave your agent without taking responsibility, that's a pretty expensive way to avoid an uncomfortable meeting.

Maybe you want to leave your agent because *the magic has gone out of your marriage* just as the magic can go out of a traditional marriage if both partners don't put energy into it. Check the discussion of Actor's Responsibilities in Chapter Seven for some ideas on how to infuse some life into the partnership. If you are both willing to save the alliance, it will take a lot less energy and resourcefulness than to go through that *just learning to get to know each other* period involved in any new relationship.

• *The bottom line is you're not getting work. It doesn't make any difference what the reason is. If you're not getting work, you have the right to leave and if you're smart, you will leave.*

Beverly Anderson
Beverly Anderson

Don't Wait Until It's Too Late

Just like anything else, if something is bothering you, speak up. Candor comes easily to very few people. We all want to be liked and it's hard to confront the situation. If you are not going out, call your agent and tell him you are concerned. He knows as well as you that you are not going out. Ask him if there is anything you can do. Ask if he has heard any negative feedback. But, whatever you do, don't just start interviewing and badmouthing your agent. If you're upset at anybody — it's dishonest to talk to bystanders about it instead of the target of your dissatisfaction.

• *Early on, at some moment, discuss problems with the agent. There are actors who hide in their kitchens, angry because they have not had auditions. By the time they can't stand it any longer, they call and tell you they're leaving. We're not omniscient; we don't know sometimes what is happening or not happening. We have meetings every week at the office and discuss all the clients and we might know someone is dissatisfied. But even if we miss it, you are obliged to come in and speak to your agent, not an*

*assistant, because you are signed by the agent. Then we'll
discuss it. We'll have a discussion and try to solve it.*
                                        Fifi Oscard
                                        Fifi Oscard Agency, Inc.

If you do wait too long and it's too late for a talk or you
talked and it didn't help, at least leave with a little class.
Even though it might be uncomfortable, get on with it:

• *I would be very upset if someone with whom I've had
a long relationship fires me by letter. I think it would be
the ultimate rudeness, ingratitude, lack of appreciation, for
the work I've done. Get past the guilt. The embarrassment. I'm owed a certain consideration. Deal with it. I
understand the difficulty, but that's not an excuse.*
                                        Phil Adelman
                                        The Gage Group

So be brave — you owe him that. Go in and meet with
your agent. Explain that, for whatever reason, it's just not
working. No need for long recriminations. No excuses.
Not, *My wife thinks* or *My manager thinks.* Simply say,
*I've decided that I am going to make a change. I
appreciate all the work you have done for me. I will miss
seeing you but it just seems like the time to make a change.
I hope we'll see each other again.* Write your own script,
this is just a direction for you to go.

No need to be phony. If you don't appreciate what the guy
has done and don't think he's done any work, just skip it.
Talk about the fact that you think the relationship is not, or
is no longer, mutually rewarding. Leave your disappointment and anger at home. Be straightforward and honest
and you'll both be left with some dignity. You may see
this person again and with some distance between you, you
might even remember why you signed with him in the first
place. Don't close doors.

If you are leaving because your fortunes have risen, it is even harder. The agent will *really* be upset to see you and your money leave. Also, your new-found success has probably come from his efforts as well as yours. But if you are really *hot* and feel only CAA, ICM, etc., can handle you, then, leave you must.

Tell him you wish it were another way but the vicissitudes of the business indicate that at a certain career level, CAA and peers have more information, clout, and other stars to bargain with and you want to *go for it*. If you handle it well and if he is smart, he will leave the door open. It has happened to him before and it will happen to him again. That doesn't make it hurt less, but this is business. He will probably just shake his head and tell his friends you have gone crazy and that: *This isn't the same Mary I always knew. It's gone to her head.*

He has to find some way to handle the rejection just as you would if he were firing you. It will not be easy to begin a new business relationship, but you are *hot* right now and the world is rosy.

Wrap Up

Questionable reasons for leaving
✓ no recent work
✓ manager pressure
✓ agent disinterest

Better remedies than leaving agent
✓ learn to communicate better with your agent
✓ take a class, study with a coach
✓ do a showcase
✓ court casting directors
✓ put your own project together

Clearcut reasons for leaving
✓ lack of respect
✓ dishonesty
✓ lack of communication
✓ differing goals
✓ personality differences
✓ sudden career change for better *or* worse

Speak to agent
✓ before things get bad
✓ before interviewing new agents

Kinds of Representation

Assuming you have your life in a fairly balanced state, have an apartment, are in class, have accumulated some credits, are involved with other actors and have analyzed the marketplace in a meaningful way, it's time to confront the next hurdle. What kind of relationship do you want with your agent?

Free-lance/Exclusive

Any sane person would want to know a potential business partner well before turning his business over to him, therefore signing the first agent you meet is not a wise business decision for either of you. If the agent is willing, it's appropriate to enter into a free-lance arrangement in which both parties are clearly considering possible future commitment.

• *Some people are better off not signing, possibly because they're the kinds of actors that agents will only submit from time to time. The agent may not feel that actor is that marketable so that you want to go out and really work hard for him.*

> Jerry Kahn
> Jerry Kahn, Inc.

• *New York is much more of a signed town than it used to be. If you are going to have a career, you really should settle on someone because free-lance is not the way to go. You don't get pushed, you don't get submitted for that many things and there is no development done, let alone any marketing.*

> Gary Krasny
> The Krasny Office

In New York it is possible to have several different agents submitting you for projects. The beauty of this arrangement is that not everyone sees you in the same way, so although one agent might not think of you for a particular job, another might.

The downside is that you must spend time *agenting* yourself to various agents much as you would if you were represented by a large conglomerate, staying in touch, keeping them informed of your activities, keeping your face in front of several different agencies instead of concentrating on just one.

In order to submit your name to a casting director, Screen Actors Guild rules require the agent to *clear* the submission with the actor. If you are not at home or you are in the shower or if the line is busy, it's possible that the agent will have to send in his list without your name.

There are agents you might not feel have enough credibility for you to consider ever signing with, but if they submit you for a job and you connect with it, that's good for both of you.

Actors and agents with no real career potential may be happy with unfocused goals. Will you?

I think it's better to have a plan. You can always change it later, but a goal moves you forward just by being there. Target several agents until you begin to get a feel for who you like. That's what they are doing with you.

- *I don't sign anyone on just meeting them because I think it's a relationship. You can liken it to a marriage. There are people who might look across the street, see someone, fall madly in love, get married and live happily ever after. Sometimes it happens that way, but very rarely.*

   Usually, it's the type of thing where people have to get to know each other, compare goals, compare needs and see how they work best with each other. So a free-lance relationship with a client is the first step towards an exclusive relationship.

   I would rather work with someone free-lance for a year and a half 'til we both knew it was right to sign and then be signed for the next 30 years than sign somebody right away and then six months later break the contract. You put so much emotion in it and are so involved in it that it's better to let it build until you know it's right. So a free-lance relationship is used to build up to an exclusive relationship.

Flo Rothaker
DGRW

A signed relationship with the right theatrical agent is a worthy goal. Don't be so afraid of making the right choice that you make no choice.

Being signed can make your life a lot easier. The agent makes his choice based on his thinking you will work and help him pay his rent if he submits you for the right projects.

Once you and an agent choose each other, it is easier to stay in touch and to become a family. It behooves you to put a lot of energy into the relationship so that the agent does think of you. If you are signed and your agent doesn't think of you, there are no other agents down the line to fall back on.

If you are smart, you won't give up your own agenting

efforts just because you are signed, you'll just focus them differently. Too many actors sign and then sit back waiting for the agent to take over all professional details. The more you can do to help your agent, the better off both of you will be.

Theatrical vs. Commercial Representation

Professional expectations of commercial agents are quite different than those of theatrical agents. Although this book is focused on agents who submit actors for theater, film and television, I would like to discuss one particular aspect of the commercial agent/actor relationships that relates to theatrical representation.

Some agencies have franchises only with SAG and AFTRA that do not cover commercials. Some agencies have no franchises with SAG and AFTRA that cover actors for theater, motion picture or television. Some agents have everything.

Because commercials are so lucrative (and theater is not), some agents require your name on the dotted line on a commercial contract before they will submit you theatrically. If that is the deal someone offers you, be wary. If they have confidence in their ability to get you work in the theatrical venue, they will not require commercial participation.

Many actors who are successful in commercials find it difficult to *cross over* into theater, film, and television and sign joint agreements only to find that they are never submitted with the agencies' theatrical clients.

Commercial vs. Theatrical Success

Frequently, commercial progress comes swiftly and the actor finds he hasn't had opportunities to build the same credibility on the theatrical level as he has commercially. He doesn't realize the agent does not feel comfortable sending him on theatrical calls because of the disparity between his theatrical and commercial resume. Until the actor addresses this, signing *across the board* is not a good business decision. There are many reasons, not the least of which is the contractual commitment.

In the rules of Screen Actors Guild, if an actor has had no work in 91 days, he can void his contract with an agent simply by sending a letter to the agent plus copies to all unions advising them of *Paragraph 6* (See Glossary).

If you have been working commercially, but have not been being sent out theatrically, you might prefer to find a new theatrical agent. But, since you have been making money in commercials, you cannot utilize *Paragraph 6* to end your relationship. Think carefully about your commitments when you sign. You may have heard about other actors who *got out* of their contracts easily. I have heard of them, too. I also know actors who had to *buy* their way out of their contract with a large financial settlement.

On the other hand, if you have a successful theatrical career going and no other commercial representation and your theatrical agent wants to sign you commercially (and he has credibility in this area), why not allow him to make some realistic money by taking your commercial calls through his office?

People win commercials because they are blessed with the *commercial look* of the moment. It's easy to get cocky when you are making big commercial money, and think you are farther along in your career than you are. What you really are is momentarily rich. Keep things in perspective.

Thank God for the money and use it to take classes from the best teachers in town so that you can begin to build theatrical credibility.

It's possible to cultivate some theatrical casting directors on your own. A few are accessible. When you've done a prestigious waiver show or managed to accumulate film through your own efforts with casting directors, theatrical agents will be more interested.

It's all a process.

Wrap Up

Free-Lance
- ✓ gives actor many different submission possibilities
- ✓ requires more upkeep
- ✓ requires vigilant phone monitoring
- ✓ gives you a chance to get to know the agent

Exclusive
- ✓ more focused representation
- ✓ all your eggs are in one basket
- ✓ easier to have a close relationship
- ✓ easy to get lazy

Theatrical vs. commercial representation
- ✓ more financial rewards for commercial success
- ✓ all representation at same agency can block *Paragraph 6* protection
- ✓ takes different credits for theatrical credibility

What Everybody Wants

If you could sign with any agent in town, which one would you choose? Would ICM be right for you? Could J. Michael Bloom be the answer? Maybe you would be better off with The Gage Group? All of the agencies I just mentioned are prestigious, but that doesn't necessarily mean acquiring A instead of B would be a wise career move.

Before we start looking for the ultimate agent or agents, consider what agents are looking for.

The Definitive Client

• *I want to know either they work and make a lot of money so that I can support my office or the potential to make money is there. I am one of the people who goes for talent, so I do take people who are not big money-makers, because I am impressed with talent.*

Martin Gage
The Gage Group

Beverly Anderson told me an instructive story about meeting a prospective client and her reaction to her:

• *Sigourney Weaver asked to come in and meet me when she was with a client of mine in Ingrid Bergman's show, "The Constant Wife." She's almost six feet tall. I'm very tall myself and when I saw her, I thought,* God, honey, you're going to have a tough time in this business because you're so huge. *And she floated in and she did something else no one had ever done; She had this big book with all her pictures from Bryn Mawr or Radcliffe of things she had done and she opened this book and she comes around and drapes herself over my shoulders from behind my chair and points to herself in these pictures. She was hovering over me and I thought,* No matter what happens with me, this woman is going to make it. *There was determination and strength and self-confidence and positiveness. Nobody's ever done that to me before.*

> Beverly Anderson
> Beverly Anderson Agency

Weaver's strength comes in some portion from having a strong, successful father, Pat Weaver, producer of "The Today Show." Though many of us were not blessed with such an effective role model, it's possible and important to pick someone who is living the life you want, study them and use some of their methods in pursuit of your goal.

Weaver was also blessed with a top drawer education, another valuable asset:

- *Training is the most important thing. I get very annoyed with people. Someone is attractive, so people say,* You should be in television, *and then the actor just thinks that's going to just* happen.

> J. Michael Bloom
> J. Michael Bloom

If you want to be pursued by an agent, find out what qualities catch an agent's eye. Michael Kingman offered his provocative list:

- *His talent. To be moved. To laugh. Feelings. Somebody who has contagious emotions.*
  I'm looking for actors with talent and health, mental

health and the ability to say, It's my career and I devote my life to this. *It's an attitude, not a spoken thing. It's an attitude that* today is not the last day of my life.

Didn't Michael realize that if we had *mental health* we probably would not need to be actors?

• *I'm looking for an actor with the ability to get a job and pay me a commission. I'm looking for people who are gorgeous and don't stutter. Or if they already have credits I can use to sell them in my business.*

Beverly Anderson
Beverly Anderson Agency

• *Spark. Personality that jumps up and says,* I'm alive. *There's a personality that comes out.*

Mary Sames
Sames & Rollnick

• *I love actors that can transform, that have range, someone that you would not recognize from one role to the next. There is something very special about that. I find that very exciting. Actors who have access to a real emotional life and the ability to put that* up there.

Brian Riordan
J. Michael Bloom

• *I'm drawn to actors that I feel they are talented and have a commitment to win. I'll go through anything with an actor as long as his commitment is to win.*

Bruce Levy
Bruce Levy Agency

• *A spark. Something that's unusual. Usually from a performance. They can cool my interest by their behavior at our interview. You not only have to have the talent, you have to apply it. You can tell sometimes by the responses that they don't yet have that capacity to apply it.*

It always boils down to the talent. If somebody has a talent even though it's someone who's a drunk, you know that there's still the wonderful performance still to be gotten. On the other hand, there's, Is it worth going through all that to wait for that wonderful performance?

> Jeff Hunter
> William Morris Agency

• *Talent. And a resume that speaks for itself. I always say,* It talks to me. *The places that you have worked. The stronger your classical background. Where did they train? Yale? Juilliard? I hate to say it, but it makes a difference. It will open doors for you.*

> Mary Sames
> Sames & Rollnick

• *Beyond the intangibles, do I like the look? The quality? What really attracts me is the resume. If it's a brand new person, the training. If it's a person with experience, what they've done, who they've worked with, a certain attitude. The attitude of an actor or actress who knows himself or herself and is understanding of his position in the business, his hierarchy.*

> Alan Willig
> Select Artists

• *I like to work with people that I like as well as respect. I like to work with people who are fairly sane, fairly stable, certainly dependable, who are well trained and who have talent. A great deal of that can be communicated in the personal projection of the person.*

> Pat House
> Actors Group

• *Our first priority is acting. There's more mileage in someone who's got talent than someone who just has the look. Obviously the perfect combination of looks, talent and charisma and you've got a star. But you've got to avoid the flash in the pan. I look for a believable quality. I'm turned off by overtrained actors.*

Kenneth Kaplan
Innovative Artists

• *I want clients to come to me already prepared. To have a sense of who they are, the kind of career they're likely to have, good self-knowledge, good reality about themselves.*

Phil Adelman
The Gage Group

• *The people to whom I offer representation are actors whose work I know and whose work excites me and those I feel that I can help them chart a course that will pay off to a long term career. Our office doesn't necessarily go in for the fast buck or the easy buck, we frequently talk actors out of work that might be financially rewarding, but not career enhancing. We believe that it's not necessarily the job, it's the job after that. What will that job lead to?*

Brian Riordan
J. Michael Bloom

• *I don't care what he or she looks like. Can he talk? Because you're always burned if you sign someone whose talent you don't believe in just because of a look. I want a kid who, if he doesn't get a movie, is still willing to go and do a 10-line role in "Moliere" at the Buffalo Studio Arena just to get the credits and build the craft in the process. It may not happen at 20. It may not happen at 30. In the meantime, they're still functioning.*

Alan Willig
Select Artists

• *Most of my actors have unusual personalities and are not easy sells. I tend to find people who are a little off the beaten track or a little offbeat mentally or are physically unusual. I like a challenge. I like the creative, the inventive, the unusual. The idea of* if you want my actor, you have to hire him because nobody else does that.

Barry Douglas
DGRW

• *I like performers who see themselves clearly, who have clear ideas of who they are, what they can do and I like them to be responsive to comments, criticism and advice born of having done this since 1949. Period.*

Fifi Oscard
Fifi Oscard Associates

• *If they're older and have been in the business and don't have some career going - they're now going to be up against people who have so many more - and important - credits.*

Robert Malcolm
The Artists Group East

• *I like clients that challenge me as an agent as they are not easily typable. I think they end up having more range. Although it may be more difficult sometimes to get them seen, it's more rewarding because it's more creative for you as an agent. As agents are known for their client lists, I think that people who are very straight on probably do well with other agents.*

Peter Strain
Peter Strain & Associates

• *I love those actors who are always trying to further perfect their craft, always in class. Because of that, they always seem to be in the mainstream of working actors because they're so serious about it.*

Monty Silver
Silver, Kass
& Massetti/East

What to Look for in an Agent

• *I'd choose an agent who is compassionate, committed, that has a good reputation in terms of negotiating skills or fighting for their clients or making opportunities available to them. You have to go on a gut feeling. The environment you are sitting in is going to tell you something about the people who are working in that office, how that office feels, what you feel like sitting in that chair. If you think it's someone who is on the same wavelength as you, whether you are coming from a similar place, that's crucial.*

Brian Riordan
J. Michael Bloom

• *One of the chief factors that determines the value of an agent is the amount of information that he has available to him. It is impossible for a small agent to possess the amount of information that a large agent can. We track hundreds of projects weekly at all of the studios and networks. If a client walks in and asks about a project, I can haul out 400 pages of notes and say,* Oh yeah, it's at this studio and this is the producer and they're doing a rewrite right now and they're hoping to go with it on this date and talking to so and so about it. *I have* that *information.*

Gene Parseghian
William Morris Agency

• *If you have a choice, look hard for someone you can really trust and someone who is not sycophantic. Someone who will say to you:* You were not good last night. *Most agents won't tell you because they are afraid you will leave them. You have got to have someone you can trust. I think that when you get that person, you should trust them. I think if they give you advice and say,* Don't do this *or,* Do this, *you should listen to them. The agent should be trusted for his expertise. If you were going to have brain surgery and you asked the surgeon what he was going to do, you wouldn't say,* Well, no. I don't think you should do it that way. *You would say,* Well, okay. I'm in your hands. *You should trust until such time as you cannot trust the person, then that is the time to make a change.*

Lionel Larner
Lionel Larner, Ltd.

Getting an audition isn't necessarily the most important thing either. Is he sending you on the *right* auditions? Does he see you accurately? Do you both have the same perception regarding the roles you are right for?

• *If the actor/agent relationship were based on getting auditions for everything, then the agent would have a right to say that you must get everything I send you out on. If you don't get everything I send you on, then we have a one-sided relationship.*

Marvin Starkman
The Starkman Agency

Oh.

Reel Power written by Mark Litwak (William Morrow, New York) is a book I recommend for information about the film and television businesses. Litwak has gathered fascinating insights about skills necessary to be effective agents:

• *First, an agent must have the stamina to handle a heavy workload and be able to endure the frenetic pace in which business is conducted.* It's like working in the commodities pit, *says William Morris agent Joan Hyler.* It's hectic, *says agent Lisa Demberg,* because you can't do your job unless you're always on the phone, always talking to someone, or socializing with someone or trying to do business, or following up on the projects you've discussed.

Great agents, *says agent-turned-executive Stephanie Brody,* have enthusiasm and tireless energy. And they must be efficient. The agent is juggling 30 phone calls a day. He has to send out material, and follow up. You have to be extremely well-organized.

Second, agents must be able to cope with the vicissitudes of the business. In a certain sense it's like Dialing for Dollars, *says William Morris agent Bobbi Thompson.* Each call may be the big money. You never know. It's all a roulette wheel.

Third, an agent must be an effective salesman.

Fourth, agents must be able to discern talent.

Many top agents are very aggressive in their pursuit of deals, some would say ruthless. Says a former CAA agent, In order to be an extraordinarily successful agent you can't have any qualms about lying, cheating, stealing and being totally into yourself.

> Mark Litwak
> Reel Power
> William Morrow, NY

I was particularly struck by what Joan Hyler said about agenting being like working in the commodities pit. Frequently there is no tangible reason why the commodities market goes up or down, just as there is often no tangible reason why one actor gets a job and the other one doesn't or why one actor is singled out by the public and another one isn't. It really is "Dialing for Dollars."

Information is important, but if you don't have the same goals, it doesn't matter.

• *I had a funny looking lady come in, mid 30s, chubby, not very pretty. For all I know, this woman could be brilliant. I asked her what roles she could play, what she thought she should get. She saw herself playing Debra Winger's roles. I could have been potentially interested in this woman in the areas in which she could work. But it was a turnoff, because not only do I know that she's not going after the right things so she's not preparing correctly but she's not going to be happy with the kinds of things I'm going to be able to do for her. So I wouldn't want to commit to that person.*

Phil Adelman
The Gage Group

• *What's essential is that the goals the actor sets for himself and what the agent wants for the actor be the same. Or at the very least, compatible, but probably the same.*

If an actor walks in and I think that actor can be a star next month and the actor doesn't, it ain't gonna happen. If the actor thinks he's gonna be a star next month and I don't, it ain't gonna happen.

By ain't gonna happen, I mean it's not gonna work between us. Even though a great deal of it may be unspoken, there has to be a shared perspective.

Gene Parseghian
William Morris Agency

• *Any agent worth his salt should know what kind of advice to give in terms of* this is a good job, this is not, this is career enhancing, this is not. *But it is so difficult out there and the actor is always sort of banging his head against what seems like a door that can't be opened in some capacity, that the most important thing is to be there for the actor emotionally. No matter how you advance in your career, the stakes rise, too. Someone who was doing theater and now wants to do movies, starts doing movies and is frustrated because he is now losing out on roles to someone who is more established. The stakes just keep getting higher. I think the emotional support that comes from believing in the actor is the most important thing in helping the actor get through that process. To be excited about and enjoy the victories, but to also help cushion the defeats.*

Brian Riordan
J. Michael Bloom

- *The actor should look at the agent's integrity. He should look at the agent's client list to see if he fits in there. He should look for communication. He should look at the agent's background.*

> Meg Mortimer
> Ambrosio/Mortimer

Size

An important aspect to consider in overall agent effectiveness is size. When we speak of size in relation to agents, we are speaking of his client list, the number of actors the agent has signed for exclusive representation.

One person cannot effectively represent 100 people. It's like going to the store and buying everything you see. You can't possibly *use* everything, you're just taking it out of circulation.

It may feed your ego to be signed, *I have an agent!* but if you are not signed with a credible agent, you may just be taking yourself out of the marketplace. Better to wait until you have the credits to support getting a better agent then to sign paper with someone who doesn't have the power to represent you effectively.

Many agents believe a good ratio is one agent to 20 to 25 clients. An agency with four agents can do well by 100 or even 140 clients, but that really is the limit. Look closely at any lists that are extravagantly over this size. It's easy to get lost on a large list.

It's all very well to have stamina, discern talent, have a short list, and be a great salesman. I take that as a given, but there are two other attributes that separate the contenders from the also-rans.

Access and Stature

The dictionary defines the word access as *ability to approach* or *admittance.*

Because the conglomerate agencies have so many stars on their lists, they have plenty of *ability to approach* because, if the studios, networks, and producers do not return those phone calls, they might find the agency retaliating by withholding their important stars.

Stature on the other hand is different entirely. Webster defines the word as *level of achievement.*

Phil Adelman and Richard Astor certainly have more stature than some lowly agent at William Morris but because they don't control an equal number of important, bankable stars, they may not have as much access. Get both if you can, but if you have to choose, go with access.

The central issue is, how do you choose the agent who will provide the opportunity for you to be gainfully employed in the business?

Wrap Up

The Ideal Client
✓   has talent
✓   possesses contagious emotions
✓   displays a singular personality
✓   exhibits professionalism
✓   manifests self-knowledge
✓   shows drive
✓   is innately likeable
✓   maintains mental health
✓   is well trained
✓   boasts a good resume

The Ideal Agent
- ✓ is aggressive
- ✓ has stature
- ✓ has access
- ✓ is enthusiastic
- ✓ shares same career vision for the actor
- ✓ has an optimum ratio of actors to agents
- ✓ has integrity

Research and Follow-through

Unfortunately, agents do not send out a resume in search of clients. Even if they are looking for clients (and they are all looking for *the* client who will make them wealthy and powerful beyond their dreams), agents don't send out a list of their training, accomplishments and/or a personality profile.

Beyond their list of clients (which is not, by the way, posted on their door), there is no obvious key to their worth; therefore, it is up to you to conduct an investigation of your possible business partners.

You have taken your first step. You bought this book. I have already done lots of research for you by interviewing agents, asking about their background, looking at their client lists, in many cases interviewing some of their clients, and in general engaging in conversations with anyone and everyone in the business who might have something informed to say about theatrical agents. I've also read everything that I could get my hands on regarding agents and the way the business is conducted.

You should begin to have agent conversations with every actor you come in contact with. If you are just beginning in the business and your actor contacts are limited to your

peers, they will probably be just as uninformed as you.
Never mind, ask anyway. You never know where
information lurks. As I said in the Introduction, read this
entire book before you make any judgments about your
readiness to attract an agent or what kind of agent you seek.
Your understanding of various bits of information is
enhanced by an informed overview, so make sure you have
one. Make sure you have absorbed how the business really
works, what you have a *right* to expect of an agent, what
you can *realistically* expect of an agent, and what *your*
contribution is to the mix.

Prepare yourself as an artist and as a business person so
that you can operate on the level to which you aspire. If
your work and presentation are *schlock*, what kind of agent
is going to want you?

Get On With It

After you've digested this book once through, go back and
read the agent listing section again and take notes. You'll
learn their lineage, education, credits (clients), the size of
their list and get some idea of their style. If there is
someone that interests you, check the index to see if the
agent is quoted elsewhere in the book. Those quotes can
give you further clues as to how the agent conducts
business, views the world, and how compatible you might
feel with them.

If you read his dossier and don't recognize any of the
clients' names, that may mean his clients are respected
working actors whose names you don't happen to know or
they could be up and coming actors who have not yet
worked. You can only evaluate the agent accurately if you
know exactly what his list means. If he only works free-
lance, that tells you something, too.

If all the agent has is stars and you are just beginning, this agent is too far along for you. If the agent has bright-looking actors with no important credits, he is building his list. If you fit that category of client, perhaps you and the agent can build credibility together. It's worth a shot.

If you are an actor of stature, you will be looking for an agent that lists some of your peers. Some fine agencies have opened in the last two or three years whose names may not be as well-known as older agencies, but who have real credibility. Usually these are started by agents who interned at larger offices, learned the business, groomed some clients, and left the nest (frequently with some of the agency's choicest clients) to open their own agencies

Once you have a list of agents who have caught your attention, go by The Players Guide office at 165 West 46th Street and spend an afternoon leafing through the pages raising your consciousness by noticing the names *and* faces of clients of particular agents. Names of actors might not be enough, faces will be more revealing. Notice which agents represent the actors in your peer group. This will help you make your agent *possibility list*.

If you are a member of The Screen Actors Guild, go look at the Agent/Client listings to check out the current client lists of the agents that interest you. There is a code to delineate theatrical or commercial contract as well as the size of the list. If you have access to both SAG and The Players Guide, check both. The SAG list gives you a quick overview of size of list and names of clients. Because the Guide does not have the actors listed by agent, it's difficult to get as focused a picture of a particular agency as that presented by looking at an entire list of clients.

As your research continues, you will have fantasies about

the large conglomerate agencies. Be sure to read the
section of the book having to do with the star agencies
before you form your final opinion; There are many pros
and cons to *star representation* at various levels of one's
career.

While you are salivating, consider that most stars come to
celebrity agencies *after* a struggling independent agent
helped the actor achieve enough stature and access of his
own that the conglomerate agent felt his interest was
financially justified.

William Morris, ICM, CAA and APA do not offer career-
building services. These large corporations are there to
cash in on the profits. Although it is true that star
representation enhances some careers, it is not true in all
cases. Be sure to read Chapter Nine.

In making your agent selections, make sure you are seeking
an agent you have the credits to attract: Brad Pitts' agent is
probably not going to be interested. Make sure clients on
the agent's list are your peers. It's all very well and good
to think big but, you must walk before you run.

Don't expect an agent who has spent years building his
credibility to be interested in someone who just got off the
bus. Remember, you must effectively agent yourself until
you are at a point that a credible agent will give you a
hearing.

I met a young actor a year or so ago who had just arrived
in California. Because he has lots of chutzpa, he was able
to hustle a meeting with an agent far above him in stature.
The agent asked if there were an audition tape available.
Although he had none, the actor said his tape was in New
York and that he would send for it. He kept putting the

agent off and finally volunteered to do a scene in the agent's office. He ended up getting signed. After he was signed, he confessed there was no tape.

A year and no jobs later, the actor angrily left the agent in search of another agent. It still has not occurred to the actor that he was just not *ready* for representation on that level.

I'm sure he will manage to waste even more time before it occurs to him to spend energy studying and doing plays instead of squandering it trying to *trick* an inappropriate agent into signing him.

Who Do You Love?

At this point, you should have some idea of which agents appeal to you. Some names will keep coming up. Make a list. Even if you know you are only interested in John Kimble or Martin Gage, target at least five names. You can't intelligently make a choice unless you have something to compare. You don't know that you like Agent A best unless you have seen Agent B and Agent C.

Now's the time to ask advice from any casting directors with whom you have formed relationships. A casting director who has hired you will probably be pleased that you asked his opinion. Tell him you are *agent shopping* and that you would like to run a few names by him.

Also ask for any names he might like to add to your list. Listen to the c.d.'s opinion but remember, he has a far different relationship with an agent than you will have. Make your own decision.

At this point your research is based on style, stature,

access, size of list, word of mouth and fantasy. Let's forge ahead to face-to-face encounters.

Getting a Meeting

The best way to contact anyone is through a referral. If you know someone on the agent's list who will act as a go-between, this is good. If a casting director whose advice you have sought offers to call, this is better, but don't put the c.d. on the spot by asking. If you ask for advice about agents and he feels comfortable recommending you, he will suggest it. If he doesn't, be thankful for the advice.

Winning an Academy Award, a Tony, or an Emmy is, of course, a great door opener. What else?

If you are young and beautiful, just go drop your picture off in person (mid-week, late afternoon) looking as Y&B as possible. It is sad (for the rest of us) but true, that if you are really Y&B and can speak at all, few will require that you do much more. May as well cash in on it.

If you are smart, you will study while cashing in since Y&B doesn't linger long and you may want to work in those grey years of your 30s and beyond.

You're not Y&B? Me neither. So this is what I suggest: If you are just starting in the business or you don't have any strong credits, concentrate on classes, showcases and writing notes to casting directors asking for meetings. It's a 9-to-5 job every day: Studying, showing, meeting.

If you have graduated from one of the League Schools (Glossary) and/or have some decent credits and/or an Audition Tape (again, Glossary), and have a clear idea how you should be marketed, it's time to begin.

It's best to send a letter that precedes a picture and resume by a couple of days. Letters get read; pictures and resumes tend to sit on the *whenever I get to it* stack.

Make sure your letter is typed. State that you are interested in representation. Say that you are impressed with the agent's client list (make sure you know who is on it) and that your credits compare favorably. If you have a particularly impressive credit, mention it.

I've been asked to provide an example. Please don't use it verbatim or every agent in town will get identical letters. This is just to stimulate your thinking:

Dear Mary Smith:

I've just moved to New York from Timbuktu and am interested in representation. I have spoken to George Brown and Sheila Jones who are in my acting class. We are all studying with Jacqueline Segal. They have told me that they have worked through you.

Since I am in their peer group, I thought I might fit in with your client list. Although I am new to town, I do have a few credits. I met John Casting Director and have worked two jobs through him: "Hello Everyone" and "It Pays to Study." The parts were small, but it was repeat business and I'm compiling an audition tape.

My picture and resume will be in your office by Thursday. I'll call on Friday to see if you have a few minutes and might be interested in seeing my audition tape. I'm looking forward to meeting you.

Sincerely,
Hopeful Actor

• *Most actors send their pictures out over the weekend and they all come in on Monday and Tuesday. If he sent his on Wednesday and it came in on a Friday, it might be the only one on the agent's desk.*

Peter Beilin
Peter Beilin Agency Inc.

If you've just graduated from one of the League schools, mention this and some roles you have played. Make sure your picture and resume tell the truth and arrive when you promised them.

If your letter has piqued interest, your picture will be opened immediately. When you call (late afternoon is best), be up and be brief. Be a person the agent wants to talk to. If he doesn't want a meeting, get over the disappointment and get on to the next agent on your list.

If you want an agent on a higher level who doesn't seem interested, don't be deterred; there are many other agents on that level. If they all turn you down, then perhaps you are not as far along as you think. Don't be depressed, that just means you need to do more work on yourself until you are ready for those agents. If you feel you really must have representation at this time, you may need to pursue an agent on a lower level, but let's think positive.

• *There are clients I don't want to work with, not because they are not talented, but because I don't want to be in a constant relationship with them. They're not bad or good, they may be wonderful people, but it's not a good marriage. There is a better agent for them. You have to be able to feel you want to see it through the* ups *and downs, it's just personality. What's good for me might not be good for somebody else and vice-versa.*

Bruce Levy
Bruce Levy Agency

Try to set up meetings with at least three agents and plan all the details of the meeting.

For starters, be on time and look terrific. This is a job interview, after all. Choose clothing that makes you feel good and look successful, and that suggests you take pride in yourself. Bright colors not only make people remember you, but they usually make you feel good, too. Remember, in today's world, packaging is at least as important as product.

Go in and act like yourself. Be natural and forthright. Don't bad-mouth other agents. If you are leaving another agent, don't get into details about why you are leaving. If he asks, just say it wasn't working out. Agents are all members of the same fraternity. Unless this agent is stealing you away from someone else, he will be at least a little anxious about why you are leaving. If you bad-mouth another agent, the agent is wondering — subconsciously, at least — what you will say about *him*.

In general, don't talk too much. Give yourself a chance to get comfortable. Adjust to the environment. Notice the surroundings. Comment on them. Talk about the weather. Talk about the stock market, the basketball game or the last play you saw. That's a great topic. It gives you each a chance to check out the other's taste.

Don't just agree with him. Say what you think. If you hated it, just say it just didn't work for you. Remember, this is a first date. You are both trying to figure out if you are interested in each other.

If you've seen one of his clients in something and liked it, say so. Don't be afraid to ask questions. But use common sense.

• *Be careful. It's not what you ask, it's how you ask it.*
Harry Packwood
Harry Packwood Talent

Phrase questions in a positive vein. Discuss casting
directors that you know and have worked for. Ask what
casting directors the office has ties with. Tell the agent
what your plans are. Mention the kind of roles that you
feel you are ready for and that you feel you have the credits
to support. Ask what he thinks. Are you on the same
wavelength? Don't just *send out*, make sure you are also
receiving.

Find out how the office works. If you are being
interviewed by the owner and there are other agents, ask
the owner if he will be representing you personally. Many
owners are not involved in agenting on a day-to-day basis.

Find out office policy about returning phone calls. Are you
welcome to call? Does the agent want feedback after each
audition? What's the protocol for dropping by? Will they
consistently view your work? Will they consult with you
before turning down work? Explore your feelings about
these issues before the meeting.

If you need to be able to speak to your agent regularly,
now's the time to talk about it. Does the office have a
policy of regularly requesting audition material for their
actors at least a day in advance of the audition? Let him
know what you require to be at your best. If these
conversations turn the agent off, better to find out now.
This is the time to assess the chemistry between the two of
you.

• *What makes a good agent? Partially the chemistry
that goes on between an actor and an agent and partially*

the chemistry that goes on between the agent and the casting director. That they can communicate on an intelligent, non-whining wavelength. A good agent has to be able to not be so restricted by casting information and breakdown, so boxed in by what they read that they don't expand the possibilities. And finally, that they can get people appointments for good work.

Marvin Starkman
Starkman Agency

During the meetings, be alert for those intangible signs that tell you about a person. Note how he treats his employees; whether he really listens; body language. How he is with people on the phone. How you feel when he's speaking to you. What's the subtext?

The agent will want to know the casting directors with whom you have relationships. Make sure this information is at your fingertips so that you can converse easily and intelligently. Even if your specialty is playing dumb blondes (of either sex), your agent will feel more comfortable about making a commitment to a person who is going to be an informed business partner.

• *Morgan Fairchild came in and out of the hundreds and hundreds of actresses and actors that I have seen and had appointments with, I've never been literally interviewed by an actress,* Okay, What have you done? Where are you going? *Incredible. She interviewed me. Yes, I was turned off to a degree, but I was so impressed by her brilliant mind and her smarts that I thought to myself,* Gal, even without me, you're going to go very far. *She came in here and she knew where she was going and she interviewed me and I thought,* That's fantastic.

Beverly Anderson
Beverly Anderson

Now that you have met the agent, given focus to him and his accomplishments, office and personnel, impressed him with your punctuality, straightforwardness, drive, resume, appearance, and grasp of the business and your place within it, it is time for you to close the meeting. Make it clear that you are having such a good time you could stay all day, but you realize that he is busy and that you in fact have a voice lesson (dialect coach, dance class, have a real appointment to do something) and must be on your way.

Suggest that you both think about the meeting for a day or two and set a *definite* time for when you will get back to him or vice versa. If he asks if you are meeting other agents, be truthful. If he's last on your list, mention that you need to go home and digest all the information. He will probably have to have a meeting with his staff before making a decision. Let him know you were pleased with the meeting. Even if it was not your finest moment — or his, be gracious. After all, you both did your best.

My advice is to hurry home and write down all your feelings about the meeting and put them away for 24 hours. Then write your feelings down again and compare them. When I was interviewing all these agents, I found I would have signed with almost all of them on the spot. They are all salesmen and they were all charming. The next day I had more perspective. By then, the hyperbole seemed to have drifted out of my head and I was able to discern more clearly what had gone on.

If the agent said he would get in touch with you and he doesn't, leave it. There are others on your list. If he forgot you, do you want him as your agent? If he is rejecting you, don't insist he do it to your face.

Remember, you are choosing an agent. The qualities you

look for in a pal are not necessarily the qualities you desire in an agent.

Making the Decision

I heard a story once about Mike Nichols. He was giving a speech to the actors on opening night:

• *Just go out there and have a good time. Don't let it worry you that The New York Times is out there, every important media person in the world is watching you, that we've worked for days and weeks and months on this production, that the investors are going to lose their houses if it doesn't go well, that the writer will commit suicide and that it will be the end of your careers if you make one misstep. Just go out there and have a good time.*

I think that's the way many of us feel about choosing an agent. When I was in New York, I free-lanced much longer than was *career-appropriate* because I was afraid of making a wrong decision that could have irrevocable consequences on my career.

• *Actors feel that if they make the right choice that somehow the agent is going to make them a star and help them be successful or they're going to make the wrong choice and that's it. And that's just not it.*
    No agent can make anybody a star or make them a better actor than they are. They are only avenues of opportunity.

Joanna Ross
William Morris Agency

• *I find that actors are sometimes overly cautious. They are sometimes guided by anxiety or fear and that leads them to say,* No, I'm going to wait, *when they really have nothing to lose by signing with a particular agent who is interested in them. If it doesn't work, he can always get out of it. It's only for a year anyway. There is so much more that can be done when there is an effective responsible agent at work that sometimes it's an actor's insecurity that holds him back, and I think wrongly so.*

Gene Parseghian
William Morris Agency

There are many agents who do not share Gene's feelings. Many would rather not sign you if they feel you are not ready for a long-term commitment.

• *I've had actors I was free-lancing with say to me,* I'm going with, *I don't know, Fifi Oscard.* I'm going to try it out and if it doesn't work in six months, I'll leave. *That tells me right away that I would never sign that person.*

Harry Packwood
Harry Packwood Talent

What both of these quotes illustrate (regardless of the agent's point of view) is that the actor is questioning his own judgment. If you don't get in a position where you trust yourself and your instincts, how can you expect someone to hire you? How can you expect someone to put all their money and hard work on your judgments as an actor when you don't believe in yourself as a person?

Alan Willig put it very well: *Know thyself and trust your agent.*

Wrap Up

Research
✓ peruse <u>NY Agent Book</u>
✓ check SAG Agent/Client Lists
✓ study <u>The Players Guide</u>
✓ consult casting directors
✓ don't underestimate word of mouth
✓ have face-to-face meetings

Tools to Set Up Meetings
✓ referrals
✓ good credits
✓ awards
✓ beauty
✓ audition tapes
✓ letter
✓ picture and credible resume

The Meeting
✓ be punctual
✓ act intelligently
✓ be sure to dress well
✓ be focused
✓ know what you want
✓ ask for what you want
✓ end the meeting
✓ set up definite time for follow-up

Everybody's Responsibilities

Once you have made a decision, there are many things to do. If you haven't notified your old agent, now is the time. As I mentioned earlier, do it in person and do it with style. Say you're sorry it didn't work out.

Make it a point to speak to and thank all your agents as well as anyone else in the office for their efforts, pick up your pictures, tapes, etc. and leave. If the parting is amicable, buy your agent a drink if that's appropriate or you might want to send flowers. Send the necessary letters to the unions.

Setting Up Shop

The next stop is your new partner's office to sign contracts and meet and fix in your mind all the auxiliary people who will be working for you. If there are too many to remember on a first meeting, make notes as soon as you leave the office as to who is who and where they sit. Until you become more familiar with them, you can consult the map before each subsequent visit.

Leave a supply of pictures, resumes and videocassette tapes. Be sparing, for bringing more is always a good excuse for dropping by. Also leave lists for *each* agent of casting directors, producers, and directors with whom you have relationships. Alphabetize them if you ever want them used. Also leave lists of your quotes (how much you were paid for your last jobs in theater, film, and television) plus information about billing. The more background you give your agent, the better he can represent you.

Now the real work begins. Remember the agent only gets 10% of the money. You can't really expect him to do 100% of the work. That may be why you are leaving your old agent. You felt he didn't work hard enough. Maybe your expectations were out of line. Maybe you were lazy. Maybe you didn't keep his enthusiasm high enough. Maybe he was a goof-off. Even if that was the case before, it really doesn't matter now. What matters now is how well you and your new agent are going to function together.

90%-10%

The concept of 90%-10% is fascinating if you think about it. How many of us have resented our agents when we have been *requested* for a job and all the agent had to do was negotiate? In fact, if all our jobs were requests, would we just have a lawyer negotiate and do away with the agent altogether? Or is the support and feedback worth something?

Maybe our whole thought process about agents is incorrect. In our hearts, we really think the agent is going to get us a job. Based upon my years in the business and my research, I finally really know that the agent does not get me work. He gets my appointments, but my work gets me work. Not only by my ability to function well as an actress, but also by adjustment to my own life.

The times I have not worked as steadily have been directly

connected to my rise and fall as a person. I went into a terrible depression when my children finally left home (the first time!) I willed myself to be up, but it was just a loss that I had to mourn. During that time, I was not particularly attractive to casting directors or anybody else. Life processes must be endured. We can change agents and mates and clothes sizes, but we can't alter reality, we must experience it. Those realities are reflected in our work and enrich us as performers.

• *If you're not working because you are in your mid-life crisis, divorce, whatever, you may not be able to readily fix it, but it's up to you to assume you have a problem and set out to fix it.*

Martin Gage
The Gage Group

Although we can hope that agents are going to initiate work for us and introduce us to the casting directors, producers, directors, etc., what they are really going to do (over the span of a career) is negotiate, initiate meetings, arrange appointments when we are requested, and, hopefully, be supportive in dark moments and help us retain perspective in the bright ones. Notice I say moments. Neither state lasts as long as it seems.

Since we are getting 90% of the money (not counting Uncle Sam), we have to give up being cranky when we realize we are going to have to do 90% of the work. Since I assume you are willing to do that — if you only knew what that meant — let's talk about that.

What the Actor Can Do

• *An actor is as much in control of his career and career choices as an agent, but an actor has to do his homework. You don't just sit back and say, Oh, I've got an agent now. I can relax. Look to see what plays are coming in on Broadway and off-Broadway. Stay on top of the scene. I know that sounds trendy, but it's your business. It needs that kind of energy. To be an actor is an extraordinarily difficult job and you've got to be working all the time on your craft, on your person. That means your instrument (voice, body, technique) better be tuned. At the same time that you're working on your acting, you've go to know what is going on. Knowing what is going on is half the job.*

Mary Sames
Sames & Rollnick

• *As an agent has to outreach, so an actor has to outreach on his own career development. I've always worried about the actor who thinks, Oh, the agent will take care of it all. That can't be. The business is about contacts and about developing those contacts. Primarily if you don't have the quality to back up the contacts, you don't have a career.*

Louis J. Ambrosio
Ambrosio-Mortimer

• *In general, anything an actor can do where he can establish a line of communication with other people in the business who are going to provide him with information, that's what he should be doing.*

Jerry Kahn
Jerry Kahn, Inc.

• *Volunteer for readings with established theater companies. Always make your services available. I can't tell you how many times when a theater has gone on to produce a play, a client of mine who was available for the reading of the play (that gave them the input they needed to say we want to do this play or not) ended up getting the role. It doesn't have to be a place where you are already connected, it may be someplace where they don't know you. These theaters have large apprenticeship programs already, but I always think, why not try? Go volunteer your services anyway. Make people know. Volunteer to be a reader in an audition circumstance, because then you sit at the table and hear what the casting people and producers and directors are saying and you hear how actors shoot themselves down. It's an important learning experience.*

Brian Riordan
J. Michael Bloom

• *When an actor calls in and says,* Isn't that play (whatever the name) coming in and aren't I right for that part? *Well, it makes my job easier.*

Mary Sames
Sames & Rollnick

• *Make sure that we have enough pictures and up-to-date resumes without our having to call and ask all the time. If you are a musical comedy performer, being willing to go to an open call if we have discussed this is what you should do. It's important to keep working whether it's in a class or a workshop or a group. Always staying like a finely tuned instrument. Networking is important, but don't expect that every time your friend gets an appointment that you will too and just because you call or drop in all the time that we are necessarily going to think of you more. You don't want to become a pest. It is a business, in spite of how casual it is.*

Gary Krasny
The Krasny Office

Put yourself in the agent's position. Everyone in the world is trying to get his attention. The people who are already his clients and the people who are not. Only those people with sensitivity, creativity, and tact are going to make the appropriate impression:

• *If actors would understand that up until 11:00 or 11:15 in the mornings, agents need to organize for the day, set up what breakdowns they have to do, solve all the problems and handle the calls that came in at the end of yesterday and prepare calls that have to go out for the first part of the morning, that this is organizational time for the agents. If they can just wait until 11:15 to call to find out about their next important piece of news, they would receive a more favorable response for getting it done quicker from the agent who is going to handle that piece of business in the office. Anytime after 11:15 and before 4:30 or 5:00.*

Gary Krasny
The Krasny Office

• *Give me information I don't know about.*

Richard Astor
Richard Astor

• *Eighty percent of the scripts come from books and those books are yours to read. If you've read a book and you think the part of Joe Blow is right for you, I don't see why you don't go out and get hold of the people who have those rights and say,* Look, I read this book. I'm a fan of this writer.

Peter Beilin
Peter Beilin

• *I'm someone who encourages people to keep working. Not only on their craft, but just as a person. I think I've always been drawn to people, let's call them,* slightly neurotic *about growth. I'm a very growth-oriented person. I like that people have interests other than just being*

*insulated in the business, I guess that's because I think
acting is about what you bring from your own life
experience. You can see from the really great careers that
they are people who have a lot going on. I do have a
couple of clients once in a while that I have to get out of
the rut of sitting and waiting for the phone to ring. Some of
them have to get into a class situation. They'll feel better
in class; scene study, audition classes, work with coaches,
but I think they have to keep moving.*

Peter Strain
Peter Strain & Associates

• *Get seen. Do something to be seen because visibility
is the name of the game. You're all competing for the
attention of the casting director. You've got to do
something to make them aware of your existence.*

Jerry Kahn
Jerry Kahn, Inc

Classes are a good way to become part of the grapevine.
When you get a day job, get one that has something to do
with the business. Sell tickets at the theater or be a waiter
at Sardi's. You're supposed to be creative.

• *Be the best you can be at any given time. Study.
Showcase your talent. Do waiver theater. Make everyone
you meet a human being.*

John Kimble
William Morris Agency

Networking

I know that *networking* is a dirty word to many of you.
You say, *Oh, I'm not good at all that* or *I don't want to
get a job just because I know someone* or *I'm here for art,
not for commercialism* or some other *elevated actor* jargon

we all use from time to time to keep ourselves from testing our limits.

The most effective networking is done with your peers. You're not going to be able to pal around with Mike Nichols or Neil Simon. You *can* pal around with the *next* Mike Nichols and the *next* Neil Simon. Become involved with playwriting groups and units. If you make it your business to attend theater whenever and wherever it's happening, you will begin to notice who the writers and directors are, who are starting their careers. Focus on those whose work appeals to you. Go up to them and let them know you like their work. After you've seen their work a time or two, let them know that you are available if they even need *any* kind of help. Become involved with them in their projects. You will all grow together.

It's hard to *break in* to what seems like the *charmed circle* because people would rather work with people they already know and trust particularly when a great deal of money is at stake. And, hey, wouldn't *you* rather work with someone *you* know?

It *is* difficult behaving naturally around management if you are not their peer, but if you are well read and develop an eye and ear for what's good, you'll be able to contribute to the conversation and begin to move toward the mainstream of the business.

Do You Really Want to Work?

My background taught me to be self-effacing and that being *pushy* was a sin. When I first arrived in New York, I auditioned a lot for commercials. I'm a pretty quick study and with concentration have the ability to memorize the lines and do the audition without the script, but I never put the paper down, because I thought they would think *I really wanted the job* and that it was too pushy to let them know that. On the day that I decided to take responsibility for the fact that *I really wanted the job* and stopped holding the script, I began booking jobs. I looked up *self-effacing* in the dictionary, it means *self-obliterating. Don't <u>do</u> it.* Sir Laurence Olivier used to ask anyone working on a project whether there was anything in it for him. If Lord Olivier could admit he wanted a job, am I going to pretend I don't?

Important Details

🕾   Have a pen and paper in your hand when you return your agent's call.

🕾   Check in often.

🕾   Return calls promptly.

🕾   Get call-waiting to make sure your agent never gets a busy signal.

☞   Take picture and resume to audition.

☞   Pay attention to common sense details of keeping lines of communication open.

☞   Trust your agent and follow his advice from picture and resume to what kinds of shows to audition for.

☞   Make sure your picture is in the current edition of <u>The Players Guide.</u>

☞   Provide your agent with ample supplies of pictures and resumes, without being reminded.

☞   Go by and pick up the script before the audition.

☞   Arrive well prepared and on time at the audition
      (build in time for emergencies).

☞   Don't try to date the receptionist.

Although I'm business oriented about my career, I never
thought about the 90%-10% aspects of things until I began
researching my first book. I *did* think when I finally signed
with an agent in NY after successfully free-lancing for a
long time that my own agenting efforts were over. With
the perspective of time and research, I realize how much I
could have contributed to my career. Because I was
passive, I allowed opportunities to pass me by because I did
not educate myself. That passivity kept me from entering
the system sooner in a more meaningful way.

Some actors become angry when they have to tell their
agents how to negotiate for them. They feel the agent is
not doing his job if he has to be reminded to go for a
particular kind of billing or per diem or whatever. That's
like being angry when you have to tell your children to
study. We all need encouragement and respond to
prodding. I don't like to admit it, but I can almost always
do a better job if someone demands it. I might not think so
initially, but scrutiny usually produces better results than
one's first effort.

If the agent has it all together and does everything perfect,
great. But it's your career. It's up to you to know not
only what the union minimums are but also how you go
about getting more money and who might be getting it. It's
up to you to figure out the billing you want and to help the
agent get it. You are getting the 90%. Not only is it your
responsibility, it's a way for you to be in control of your

destiny in a business where it is too easy to feel tossed about by the whims of the gods.

Agents' expectations

Before I talk about the Agents' Responsibilities, let's get hear what agents expect from actors:

• *Loyalty. A sense of humor. I would like to think that they believe in what we are doing. And that we have a professional friendship.*

Alan Willig
Select Artists

• *One of the things I expect from actors is that they love what they do. They may not love the getting work part - but doing the work.*

Peter Beilin
Peter Beilin

• *If I sign an actor for a year, I expect (in that year) consistent callbacks. Or let's say I expect, at least, growth. I'm not going to look at somebody's track record and say,* You've been out on 50 things here and you haven't booked a job; I don't think there's anything we can do here. *It's difficult. It's very competitive. If I've believed in someone from the beginning and if I see progress, if I see growth, and if I see the potential is still there, then I'm encouraged.*

Kenneth Kaplan
Innovative Artists

• *I expect the same commitment that I am giving; that you are doing everything you can to advance your career as well. That can mean being in a class and keeping your skills honed so that whatever opportunity I am able to send your way, that you are giving it 100%. Everyone is entitled to screw up. I don't expect every client to get every job, but I expect them to give it a really good shot. And I do expect that if the actor* blew it *that he will call and tell me,* hey, I blew this. Can you talk to them. Can you explain this away, tell them I had a bad day, whatever? *It is that kind of communication going back and forth.*

Brian Riordan
J. Michael Bloom

- *I expect that they'll prepare the audition material ahead of time, they'll show up punctually, that they won't be afraid to go out on a limb and take some risks with the material, that they return my phone calls promptly.*

Gary Epstein
Epstein/Wyckoff

- *I don't expect them to get every job. Actors sometimes get embarrassed if they don't get the job. But, once an agent makes a commitment to the actor, we're not talking about three weeks or three months, we're talking, hopefully, about a long time. My commitment is for the long term because there's something in that actor that I respond to and you never know quite when it's going to break. I do have pretty much unlimited faith as long as we have communication. It's when the actor withdraws, when you don't have the communication you need, that you get into problems.*

Pat House
Actors Group

- *I expect my clients to be on time, to be prepared, to be pleasant and to do the best job he can. We do wonder what actors do for their 90% of the money. Once I get you in the door, you are on your own. I think actors should not be afraid to take control of the situation. If they want to start over, they should say so. If they want to read different sides, they should ask for it. If they want to read another character, they should go for it. If they feel they were ignored, they should say so and not complain and whine to the agent. The actor is a grown up and casting directors are not demi-gods, they are people even though they have total control. I don't mean the actor has to complain, but make known that it wasn't comfortable.*

Gary Krasny
The Krasny Office

• *Professional deportment; that they will check their service, that they will be prepared for their auditions, that they'll be prepared for interviews. The basic ABC's of being on time for interviews and reporting back, being out there to make friends.*

Marvin Starkman
Starkman Agency

• *Communication. Feedback. I want to know how the audition went the minute you leave there. Instantly. I need to know if it was sensational. I need to know if it was bad so that if I get a call from a casting director that I know how to defend my client. I don't want to get a call from a casting director and have egg on my face.*

Pat House
Actors Group

• *I expect their loyalty to me when I work hard for them. I expect them to return what I give to them; the same kind of caring that manifests itself in their work and auditions and punctuality and all those things that are important.*

Michael Kingman
Michael Kingman

• *Don't suffer in silence. Don't do that. You short change yourself as well as me. I need to know a little bit of*

*what is going on in the actor's mind. When I probe, I
frequently find out that the actor is embarrassed that he
hasn't gotten a job. I say,* Don't be silly; this isn't just for
10 minutes.

> Pat House
> Actors Group

• *A client will say,* Are you angry with me because I
didn't do so and so? *No. I'm giving you choices and
opportunities. You make the decision and I'll go along with
it. If I think it's a self-destructive point, I'll tell you. We
can talk about it, but it's your decision ultimately.*

> Tim Angle
> William Morris Agency

• *You're not going to get every part you go in for.
You're not going to get nearly every part you go in for.
But what I never want to hear is;* He was late; It was a
slovenly audition. *I don't even mind hearing,* She didn't do
well. *What I don't ever want to hear is;* He didn't pick up
the sides; She was ten minutes late. *All those things that
eventually hurt. Be prepared. If I'm putting my reputation
on the line to get you the appointment, then put your
reputation on the line enough so that I'm not looking like a
fool for sending you in on it.*

> Alan Willig
> Select Artists

The agent is putting *his* reputation on the line by sending
you in. And in *every* audition, you are putting *your*
reputation on the line by the quality of your work:

• *My job is to get the appointment. Your job is to show
up, sell yourself and do your thing.*

> Martin Gage
> The Gage Group

What the Actor Has a Right to Expect

As I mentioned in Chapter One, all we want an agent to do for us is get us meetings for projects we are right for. This very simple thing we are asking agents to do involves all the things I just mentioned that actors need to do; being informed and professional, networking, staying visible, and communicating.

As we maintain our credibility by giving consistently good readings, the agent maintains his credibility every time we make a good showing. The agent has to build trust with the buyers so that when he calls and says, *See K Callan, you won't be sorry*, that the casting director knows he won't. Then, if K Callan gets the job, the agent must to be ready to do a wonderful job of negotiation, one that will make the actor (and the agent — he does get 10%) happy and at the same time make the casting director feel he got a bargain.

• *If the casting director gives me 20 minutes to submit people, I may call and say,* I don't need that much time, I only have two people. *I don't want to send people who are not right for it. I don't want to waste the casting director's or my client's time.*

Lionel Larner
Lionel Larner, Ltd.

So the agent has all our responsibilities and more. Essentially the agent must maintain relationships with all the with his clients and with the buyer. He has a vested interest in keeping the buyer happy so that he can have return business, but no buyer hires you because he likes your agent. If you do a fantastic job, you make your agent look good *and* you make the casting director look good. And if you don't, you're not the only one who is unhappy.

What the Actor Doesn't Have a Right to Expect

A successful actor/agent relationship is no different than any other relationship. No one likes to be presumed upon:

⊗   It is not okay to call your agent at home other than in an emergency.

⊗   It is not okay to drop by the office at any time and expect the agent to be available to talk to you.

⊗   It is not okay to expect your agent to deal with your personal problems.

⊗   It is not okay to arrive late (or very early) for your meetings.

⊗   It is not okay to expect to use the agent's phone for personal calls.

⊗   It is not okay to hang around with the agent's auxiliary people when they are supposed to be working.

⊗   It is not okay to bad-mouth the agent to others in the business. If you've got a gripe with the agent, take it up with him.

⊗   It is not okay to interview new agents while your old agent thinks your relationship is swell.

⊗   It is not okay to call and say: *What's happening?*

⊗   It is not okay to expect the agent to put all the energy into the relationship.

Although many agents will be amenable to your dropping
by, using the phone, and visiting with the secretary, etc.,
it's best not to take these things for granted. After all, you
want these people to be free to be doing business for you.

If you are not feeling confident about yourself, go to class,
talk to a friend, a shrink, whatever, but don't burden your
agent with that information. Will he feel like using up his
credibility calling casting directors and telling them that you
are the best actor since Robert Deniro when you can't even
get out of bed?

If you are not up to auditioning well, tell your agent you
are sick and postpone or cancel the audition. You are not
only not going to be performing well enough to get the job,
but people will also lose confidence in you and it will be
harder to get the buyer to see you next time.

The point is, agents really are there to get you appointments
and to negotiate. I believe you also have a right to expect
them to consistently view your work and to consult with
you before turning down work. Their advice regarding
career moves is one of the things you are paying for, as
well. They are a conduit to and from the casting director
and, as such, should convey feedback honestly about the
impression you are making.

Make it clear you are ready to hear the bad with the good
and you would prefer he express it in a constructive
manner. Not *You did lousy,* but *You were late* or *You were
not prepared* or *The casting director said your energy was
down.* Let him know that you want to remedy any
problems, but that you need to know what they are. It's
hard to assess auditions accurately without feedback.

Some agents will give you advice about pictures, resumes,

hard to assess auditions accurately without feedback.

Some agents will give you advice about pictures, resumes, dress, etc., but, unless you are just starting in the business or have just come to the East Coast marketplace, established agents assume you have that all in tow and your relationship will suffer if they constantly feel you are asking for their time in matters that are basically your responsibility. That said, you may ask if your agent is interested in having input regarding pictures. This is the agents' sales tool (along with an audition reel) and he may feel strongly that pictures are one area where he wants to take time to advise you. Sometimes I take my pictures to my agents for advice and sometimes I don't. My agents are busy and since they haven't made of point of asking me to always consult them, I, frequently, do it on my own. And *sometimes*, they don't think I made the best choice.

If I were writing a book I thought agents would read, I would suggest that periodically they call the actor in (whether the career is going well or not) and ask the actor to rate the agency. Is the actor feeling comfortable? Cared for? Serviced properly? An annual mutual rating wouldn't be a bad idea. Is the actor doing his part? Is feedback good? Pictures and/or resume need updating?

At contract renewal time, perhaps the agent himself (instead of an assistant) would call and say:

K, how are you? It's contract renewal time, I'd love to have you stop by and have a cup of coffee with me (lunch?) and have us talk about our relationship. We're still happy, we hope you are, but I'd like to get some input from you on what kind of job we're doing. Come in. We'll talk. We'll celebrate your contract renewal.

by the agent *before* my big break.

Staying in Touch

- *Be seen* visually *by your agent on a regular basis.*
  John Kimble
  William Morris Agency

Ric Beddingfield at Gold/Marshak in Los Angeles says actors should make it a point to be seen by their agents once a week. Although most agents agree grudgingly that it is necessary for actors and their agents to be in constant contact, most agree that they hate to get a phone call that says *What's going on?* They translate that into *Where's my appointment?* It's kind of like when you were little and your mom said, What are you doing, when she meant, *Is your homework done?*

If you think about it from that perspective, perhaps you can find a way to have a conversation that does not make the agent feel defensive. If you are calling to say you've just gotten a good part in a Waiver play or just begun studying with a new teacher or, *Hey, did you see the new play at The Public? It's great, don't miss it,* the agent is going to be a lot happier to hear your voice or see your face.

The Gersh Agency encourages it's clients to stay in touch:

- *The new actors we encourage by getting to know them, taking them out and talking to them. We use excuses to get them here at first; come and redo your resume, come and look at your pictures, come read scripts.*
  We encourage clients to stop in all the time. We feel the office should be kind of a stopping ground, a resting place for people who are out on auditions. I don't mean that we have a lobby crowded with unemployed actors, but

*certainly stopping by once in a while is fine. They know me
well enough that if I'm busy, they don't come in. If I'm not
busy then they come in and talk.*

Ellen Curren
Gersh Agency New York

Some agents don't feel that way. One of my favorite
quotes is from an agent in Los Angeles who said,

• *My worst day is when I talk to more clients than
buyers.*

• *I'm glad to have actors call in, but I do ask them to
use discretion. Actors forget that every time I'm taking a
call, that is less time I have to be agenting. If you are
calling about a project, leave a message. They don't have
to talk to me. The more time they leave me alone, the more
time I have to agent. Please don't call and say,* What's
going on? *That makes me crazier than anything else.*

Mary Sames
Sames & Rollnick

I agree with Mary. I understand that she needs her time to
agent. On the other hand, if I'm just going to leave
messages all the time, when are we ever going to have a
relationship? We don't have to go to dinner, but I do like
to see my agents often enough that I feel comfortable with
them. My agents and I have known each other for years
and years and we really do feel *like family* with each other,
but just as with your own family, if you don't put energy
into the relationship, you begin to have nothing to talk
about when you call.

A few non-obnoxious ways to stay in touch include
communication when you drop off pictures and resumes.
Don't just leave them with the receptionist. Call ahead and

say that you are going to drop off new pictures and want to pop in say *hi* or ask the receptionist if you can just stick your head in once you get there. Late afternoon is best.

You can just be *in the neighborhood* and drop by to show a new wardrobe or haircut. Then be sure to do that; just poke your head in. Don't sit down unless asked and if asked, stay no more than five minutes. Be adorable and leave. If you are depressed and need to really talk, call ahead and see if your agent has time for you. Suggest a cup of coffee after work. Suggest a snack in the middle of the afternoon and bring goodies. Everyone is happy to see a treat in the late afternoon. Since everyone is on a diet, bring something beautiful and healthy.

Speak to *everyone* in the office and call each by name. Make the effort to know your agents and their support staff on a person to person basis. Learn something about each one of them, so that you will have something to say to them that is not about *you* and/or the business.

• *The worst words are* calling to check in. *If you want to remind me of who you are, I always tell people to send me postcards. And send me a postcard that says something. Don't just send a postcard that says you are checking in. Tell me you got a job and are going off to do something or whatever. Don't tell me,* Look I got this job; if you had sent me, you'd have gotten the commission. *Tell me you had a couple of callbacks for something or that you just got down to the wire on something, things that tell me abut progress.*

Flo Rothacker
DGRW

• *We don't need phone-ins. We don't have the manpower. We encourage people to let us know when they are in showcases. Obviously, we can't go to all of them. We usually end up picking reliable ones. By that, I mean reliable by reputation - of the theater, quality of production, the kind of cast they usually attract, and also the material. We stay away from showcases that do a lot of Shakespeare, a lot of the classics. I don't think they're going to show the actor in anything we could sell them for.*

Peter Strain
Peter Strain & Associates

It does take two energy-expending components to make any merger work. The agent must work hard for you all the time and you need to deliver *all the time*. If you don't stay abreast of what's in town, what shows are on television that might use your type, what you got paid for your last job, which casting directors you have met, who your fans are, and if you are late to appointments and ill-prepared, the agent is going to get cranky. If he doesn't drop you, he'll stop working for you. Worse, you'll get work anyway and he won't feel able to drop you; he'll just hate you.

If you are diligent and do everything you can do for your own career and consistently give your agent leads that he doesn't follow up on, then you're going to get cranky and leave.

It takes two.

Wrap Up

Details
- ✓ officially notify old agent that you are leaving
- ✓ take pictures, resumes, tapes, quotes, billing, etc., to new agents office
- ✓ meet everyone in the office
- ✓ make map

90%—actor's part

✓   stay professionally informed
✓   network
✓   follow through
✓   communicate
✓   make informed suggestions
✓   get in a good acting class
✓   have call waiting/dependable answering machine or service
✓   check in and return calls promptly
✓   stay visible
✓   be loyal
✓   pick up the sides
✓   be punctual
✓   do *great* auditions
✓   give and get feedback

10%—agent's part

✓   arrange meetings with casting directors, producers and directors
✓   arrange auditions
✓   negotiate
✓   network
✓   maintain credibility
✓   communicate
✓   make informed decisions
✓   stay professionally informed
✓   return phone calls promptly
✓   guide career

Self-Knowledge

Buckminster Fuller says if all the wealth of the world were redistributed equally, that in 25 to 50 years, there would be the same distribution of wealth we have today because not everyone would use the money wisely. He says this is a law of physics.

That same law applies to actors. If all actors had the same talent and training, some would *still* be unemployed, because talent and training are the *minimum* requirements for survival. When people use the word *talent*, they usually refer to *acting* talent, but other talents govern how effective the acting talent can be. Efficient, stable, work-oriented actors will always win, over self-destructive, lazy actors who are chronically late and think the world owes them a living.

When you hear about all the starving actors vying for five agents and one part, you can screen out many of those thousands. They won't be your competition because they have no appetite for taking care of business. It doesn't matter if there are only five agents and one part as long as you get the part and one of the agents.

I asked agents what was the most important *single piece of advice* they would like to give to actors who would read this book. 75% of the New York agents said:

Know Which One You Are

Don't expect to play Sharon Stones' parts if you look like Joan Cusack. When I first arrived in New York, I did everything I could lest I be mistaken for the middle-class lady from Texas I was. I wanted to be a *New York lady*. What I didn't realize, Texas accent not withstanding, was that my very middle-classness is what I have to sell. I *have* played ladies who went to Vassar, but more often, they can and *will get* a lady from Vassar for those parts.

I'm an authentic lady from Texas who has raised three children and had various life experiences before, during and after. There is nobody else who has all my particular components. If I don't prize what is uniquely me and find a way to tie that to a universality of the life experience, not only will I not work consistently and honestly, but my life will be a mess as well.

I asked Gary Krasny to list *actor mistakes*:

- *Not being in touch with who they are, what type they are, their limitations, their strengths, their weaknesses, their inability to grasp the fact that they can't be seen for every thing in town and that just because a friend gets an appointment doesn't mean he will get one, too. They have to figure out what they are right for and what they are best at; not knowing their own limitations.*

Gary Krasny
The Krasny Office

- *Realistically, they've got to really look. If they want to be on a soap, they should know there are requirements to being on a soap. Training. Training and a certain look.*

Each soap has a different style and a different look.
Someone says, I want to be on a soap *and I say,* Which
one? *and the actor doesn't know what they are or what*
soap hires what kind of person. They have to do their
homework.

William Schill
William Schill Agency

• *A lot of people are just totally unrealistic. They're*
either young and unattractive and/or overweight and
inexperienced. And they do have a chance of being an
actor, but when you look like that, it's not going to happen
for 20 or 25 years. They'll have to be a character person.
They have a fantasy of acting and they haven't done
anything about it. They must do the work, they must learn
the craft.

Lionel Larner
Lionel Larner Ltd.

• *Objectivity. An actor can develop objectivity. It's*
very difficult. I don't know how one does it, but one has to
have a certain objectivity about oneself and not freak out in
certain situations that are difficult; in a crisis, not to allow
your emotional life to carry you over into decisions that are
not correct decisions. Decisions have to be weighed over a
period of time and not in hysteria.

Jeff Hunter
William Morris Agency

• *Actors either don't know the realities of the business*
or their own limitations and how they are perceived. This
happens less with younger actors. It happens more with
more established actors who are doing television series and
want to be movie stars. Not having a realistic sense of
where they are in their careers, how they are perceived,
what they really are capable of or not capable of. It's hard

*to reason with an actor who doesn't have an accurate sense
or sensibility of who they are. A person like that ends up
tying themselves up in such knots over the fact she is Kathy
Najimy and not Sharon Stone that she becomes incredibly
frustrated and ends up leaving her agent. She never takes
responsibility for it and ends up saying,* Well, if I had a
different agent *and ends up leaving the agent. And still
doesn't end up being Sharon Stone.*

Brian Riordan
J. Michael Bloom

• *They don't understand how the business works. I
can't really blame them. All they want to do is act and
everything seems to get in the way of doing their piece. I
feel bad about that.*

*They don't understand the reality of what it takes to
get a project on, the amount of money involved, the fact
that everybody involved is scared to death for their lives,
their reputations, and that when somebody comes walking
through the door, they better be less scared than these
people are or they're not going to get the job. Nobody's
going to trust them with the money and the responsibilities
that go with some of the roles.*

Marvin Starkman
The Starkman Agency

Sometimes we do get the idea that insecurity is charming
and that admitting it is even more endearing. We
announce to the buyers at an audition that we are petrified
of being there and that, because of this, we are sure we
won't do our best. Really? When *had* you planned to do
your best? In front of 5,000 people? Is that going to be
easier?

For the record, insecurity is not charming. It is not
appealing. And it is certainly not going to inspire the

people with money to trust you with the responsibility of *carrying* their project. If you find yourself in a continuing state of anxiety, there is either something thing wrong with you physiologically or you are *getting off* on it. If you enjoy being a basket case, take responsibility for that. This can be a marketable attribute if you prepare yourself to play those kinds of roles. Otherwise, get yourself together and start *behaving* as though you have complete confidence in your abilities. Pretty soon, you won't be pretending anymore.

In Los Angeles, there is a radio psychiatrist I frequently listen to on the way to auditions. When someone calls him and confesses he is obsessing about something, the shrink says: *Give it up. Get over it.* If you don't have an investment in staying in a state of anxiety, you *can* let all that go. The mind is powerful.

Driving away from yet another rejection, a friend of mine started to totally lose it. He was frightened. He felt he would never work again and that he had never been talented in the first place - every actor's secret fear. Finally, he pulled his car over to the side of the road and talked to himself,

• *Wait a minute. You are not starving. Your children are not dope addicts. You are making a living, though not as much as you want, in the business you love. What is your problem? Just that you are not a star? Just that you don't work every day? I'm going to make a deal with you. Three years from this day, all your dreams are going to come true.*

Therefore, you can start enjoying your life. Go back and take some classes again and become more assured. Take the dialect class you always wanted to take. Go to the gym — create a great body.

Get on with your life. You are talented, trained, professional, well thought of in the business and a person of integrity. You are missing your life mewling and puking right here on Sunset Boulevard.

By managing to be his own shrink, this actor tells me he's never been happier, auditioned better or worked more. He doesn't get upset if not chosen because he's *decided* he's okay.

Milton Katselas is a well-regarded director who is also a highly thought of teacher in Los Angeles. I sat in on a class of his when a working actor complained that he just had to keep it together a little longer because *the payoff* was just around the corner. Milton stopped him and asked, *What's just round the corner?* The actor answered, *The payoff.* Milton smiled at the actor and said, *No. The payoff is now.*

All we have is now. If you are not fulfilled by the now, get out of the business. If the payoff for you is the big bucks, the Tony or the Academy Award, change jobs now. You will miss your whole life waiting for the prize. If you are unlucky enough to get the prize with this mind-set, you will find you are just the same unhappy person who now has an Academy Award, that you were the day before.

Mental health, balance and self esteem are necessities:

• *People who are too insecure to ask for an agent just might not make it.*

> Barry Douglas
> DGRW

• *An actor is in a very tough position because he has to believe in himself in order to produce. On the other hand, there's a point where an actor believes so much in himself that he's unrealistic. There's a dichotomy between self-confidence and self-infatuation.*

Jeff Hunter
William Morris Agency

• *The most important person to like you is the audience. Before the audience can like you, the producer has to agree to pay your salary. Before the producer agrees to pay your salary, the director has to agree to work with you.*

Before the director can agree to work with you, odds are, the casting director has to bring you in and say you're right for the role. Before the c.d. can say you're right for the role, an agent has to submit you. Before any of these people get to see you, the first person who has to say, I'm good, *is the actor.*

If you're not going to be confident enough to take a risk with a piece of material, to look at a piece and say, Ah, I can expose the humanity of this character; I can develop the creativity of this moment of the theater or film or television better than anyone in the universe. I am the first person on this. *If the actor doesn't believe that, no one else will. It's got to come from the actor first.*

Barry Douglas
DGRW

• *Don't take it personally. If you don't get a job, that's not indicative of how good you were. There are so many things that come into play; how old they were, how tall they were, how dark they were, how light they were, if their voice quality didn't make the match they were looking for with the other voice qualities and on and on and on. They could be the best of the job and still not get it. Some actors are crushed. They know they did a brilliant job.*

I hear from the casting director that they did a brilliant job and they don't get it. An actor has to have resiliency. It's a hard thing to have. He has to do a lot of work on himself personally. In order to be a good actor, one must keep oneself vulnerable and if you are vulnerable, you will take it personally.

You must get off it, *go away from it, move on to the next thing. Be crushed and get on with it. Don't carry it with you. If you carry it to the next thing, you will be pulled under.*

Bruce Levy
Bruce Levy Agency

• *Actors have to look in the mirror and assess themselves as to persona and look inside their soul and assess themselves as artists to see if they have what it takes on that level and then to see if they have the stamina. It's a wicked business.*

Louis J. Ambrosio
Ambrosio/Mortimer

Reality

In a business of fantasy, the actor who makes it must maintain perspective and remain excruciatingly realistic about himself and the business.

• *Realize that everybody's career is different. Some people may be 25 years old and may be a star and then others may not make a dime until they are 50. They have to relax and not think about being a big Broadway star or a big movie star. You have to be a constant actor, not be so concerned with success. You can't say,* Well, my friend is doing a Long Wharf show and I'm just doing off-Broadway. *Everybody's career is different.*

Harry Packwood
Harry Packwood Talent

●   *It's a business of survival. Your turn will come if you're good. It may not come as often as it should, but it'll come. We discover that they eventually find you. So you can make it if you can survive and you can only survive if you have no choice.*

If you go into the business and say, Well, I'll do this for five years and I'll see what it's like or I'll do something else, *if you have something else you can happily do, do it. It's only the people who are so committed, so desperate in some way that they'll put up with the humiliation, that they will allow themselves on ten minutes notice to be there, they'll allow themselves to be open and vulnerable, to still expose who they are and still be strong and closed enough to survive that kind of open wound life, they're the only ones who are going to make it, the people who have no choice.*

Barry Douglas
DGRW

●   *Be aware of what you look like; what your strengths and weaknesses are. If you can't sing, don't tell your agent you can.*

Alan Willig
Select Artists

●   *This is a business that rightfully or wrongfully, prefers prettier people. The prettier person gets the second look. Ultimately, it's a reflection of what the audience wants.*
Tim Angle
Don Buchwald & Assoc.

●   *Just because you don't get the job doesn't mean you're not good. There are many variables that you have no control over. An actor commits to a difficult life, he can't get a job and expect to be employed for five years like other people do. In other worlds if you get a job and do well, you can expect to work for years. That is not an actor's life.*

Bruce Levy
Bruce Levy Agency

• *Don't look at other actors' careers from the wrong end of the telescope. Don't look at what they did and think,* Oh, they just went from one thing to the next. It was just this inevitable golden path and they just had to walk along it.

Tim Angle
Don Buchwald & Assoc.

• *I believe you will arrive at the success point you are intended to arrive at simply by working hard, not faltering and having confidence that it does happen. It does happen. You get where you're supposed to get in our business.*

Fifi Oscard
Fifi Oscard Agency, Inc.

• *It used to be that there was a real sense of building a career. I'd go to a showcase or go to a school and see somebody and sign him or her; the process would begin. I'd send them to a few people, they'd get an off-Broadway show, maybe a small part, or they'd get an understudy in a Broadway show, maybe her third year a supporting part, maybe her fourth year really get noticed, maybe in the fifth year nibbles from the movies. And you'd watch progression happen and the actor would be ready for it when the break would come. They'd paid their dues. Now you can make an impact in any medium and it doesn't mean a thing. The* whatever happened to *is now constant.* Where is so-and-so who won a Tony in 1978 or an Oscar? *There's no progression in theater. There isn't even any in film or television. You're in a series that flops, the studio blames you. There are no longer any steps. It used to be - even*

*though we depend on the whims of the gods - that if an
actor did his work and didn't screw up his career, he would
at least work, maybe not be a star, but have a career - at
least be able to say,* I work at this. *Well, that's not true
anymore.*

Alan Willig
Select Artists

I disagree, I think the difference is that now, while you are
paying your dues, you might get a job that gives you
visibility and money for a month or even a year or two that
makes you think you are further along in the process than
you are. Once your series (only one job, after all, no
matter how long it lasts) or movie or play is over, you are
not *visible* in that show business way and you may think
your career is over just because employment opportunities
are no longer so high profile.

Visibility, actually is a double edged sword. In television,
particularly, the buyer prefers a talented new face over an
actor who has just finished a series. Frequently a semi-
famous face finds itself unemployed because the buyer
thinks it's too identifiable with a previous show.

Consistent Work

The task that takes more time than anything else is looking
for and winning the work. Even two-time Academy Award
winner, Sally Field says it isn't like she thought it would
be. She's constantly reading scripts, looking for things.
Then, when there is something wonderful to do, she still
has lots of competitors.

That's depressing, isn't it? It *never* lets up. I think
sometimes that if they just gave me all the jobs, that I might
lose interest and leave the business. I certainly wouldn't

mind putting *that* one to the test.

Assess Yourself & the Marketplace

Begin to actively assess which one you are. Are you a young character person? A juvenile? Someone who is right for a soap? In order to see yourself clearly within the framework of the business, study the marketplace. View theater, television, film with distance. Notice what kinds of actors consistently work. What is common to the people that work? Notice who is like you and who is not. Keep a list of roles you have seen that you realistically think you would have been right for.

As you become more informed about the business, you will begin to perceive the *essence* of people and notice its role in the casting process. More important than the look is essence. The thing that is the same in the many diverse roles of Robert De Niro is the strength of spirit.

Practice thinking like a casting director. Identify the essence of Alan Rickman, Billy Crystal and Whoopi Goldberg. Cast them in other people's roles. What would have been the effect if Sissy Spacek had played Whoopi's part in "Ghost?" What if Billy Crystal played Woody Allen's part in "Annie Hall?"

Impossible? Yes, but this exercise will help you understand why you will never be cast in certain roles and why no one else should be cast in your parts when you figure out what those parts are.

Work on your appearance. Does it match your essence? Another responsibility you have is to be the best looking you that you can be, given what you came with. As Tim Angle says elsewhere in the book, the business gravitates toward prettier people. Just as in life. Getting upset about that fact is like throwing a fit because the sun shines in your window every morning and wakes you up. Get a shade. If you are not pretty, be clever.

There is an inspiring feature on the late Ruth Gordon in the Los Angeles Times that I reread in dark moments:

• *Two things first. Beauty and courage. These are the two most admired things in life. Beauty is Vivien Leigh, Garbo; you fall down in front of them. You don't have it? Get courage. It's what we're all in awe of. It's the New York Mets saying,* We'll make our own luck. *I got courage because I was five-foot-nothing and not showgirl-beautiful. Very few beauties are great actresses.*

> "The Careerist Guide
> to Survival"
> Paul Rosenfield
> The Los Angeles Times
> Calendar Section
> April 25, 1982

The Process

• *Nobody changes the rules. What you can do is play the game for what you want or at least toward your ends. Nobody will force you to do work that you find insulting or demeaning. You have to figure out the rules in order to figure out how to play the game. You have to figure out what is a variable and what's not.*

If actors would take the time to put themselves in the shoes of the people they're dealing with, they would very quickly figure out what's reasonable and what's not. Actors don't understand why Equity Principal Auditions are a bad idea.

The reason is that no one can look at 250 people

audition in a single day and give an accurate response. That's one of the reasons they only see 40 people for a role. Knowing that isn't going to make your life easier but it means it's not like some arbitrary system where God touches this person and says, You get to audition, and you, as the untouched person, sit there wondering.

If you think about a director casting a play and you understand what that director will have to do to cast it as well as possible, at least you know what you're up against. It's not some vague, amorphous obstacle. It's not fair but at least it makes sense.

What you know *is never as bad as your imagination. If you know what you're up against, it can be difficult, but at least it's concrete. What you don't know, your imagination turns into,* Everyone in the business knows I shouldn't be doing this. I'm just not talented. *It's like conspiracy theories.*

Tim Angle
Don Buchwald & Assoc.

● *We'd all be a lot better off if actors knew what went on behind the agent's door. That it's actually a lot more simple and that there's not as much mystery about what happens between the agent and the casting director and the director and the producer as a lot of actors want to weave myths about. Most of the time, the actor is just not right for the part.*

Kenneth Kaplan
Innovative Artists

● *Careers are like pyramids. You have to build a very solid base. It takes a long time to do it and then you work your way up. No single decision makes or breaks a career. I don't think actors are ever in a position where it's the fork in the road or the road not taken where it's,* Now, okay, your career is now irrevocably on this course. Too bad, you could have had that.

If an actor looks at another person's career and says, I don't want that, *he doesn't have to have it. People do what they want to do. It's like people who are on soaps for 20 years. Well, it's a pretty darn good job, pays you a lot of money and if you're really happy, great. But if you're an actor who doesn't want to do that, you won't. Nobody makes you sign a contract. Again. And again. And again.*

Tim Angle
Don Buchwald & Assoc.

• *Be concerned with the process, not just the end result. The process is really important. At our office, we like them to be talented, yes, but we like people to train, to be in good shape, always in a good frame of mind or try to be. They need to use whatever facilities they can to promote that.*

Ellen Curren
Gersh Agency New York

• *Every decision you make is a risk because it's all collaborative and it can all stink. Every play at the Public is not a good play. Every television series isn't a piece of junk. People make decisions based on what price they want to pay, because there is a price.*

If you don't want to work in television, there's a price. If you want to work in television, there's a price. If you want to work in New York in theater, there's a price. You have to decide if that's worth it and it's an individual decision, not a moral choice. It shouldn't be something you have to justify to anybody but yourself.

It's not about proving to your friends that you're an artist. It's about what's important to you at that moment. People can do two years on a soap and that can give them enough money to do five years of theater. And that's pretty important. It depends on why you're doing it and what you're looking to get out of it, what is the big picture. And nobody knows it but you.

Tim Angle
Don Buchwald & Assoc.

The second favorite piece of advice agents wanted to impart to actors concerned marketing and professional behavior.

• *I wish actors knew more about business things. It's hard. When people have gone through school for four years or eight years and have gone through wonderful conservatory training, very seldom is any attention paid to the business aspect. People who have been working four to six years on their craft are suddenly here in New York where it's 50% craft and 50% business and they're not prepared and not knowledgeable about those situations. Simple things like pictures, resumes, answering services, finding out about things they're right for. It's all business things.*

Flo Rothacker
DGRW

• *One of the things I wish actors knew about was the business part of the business. A little bit more about their own union rules and regulations so that every time you get an actor a job you don't have to explain to them what the contract entails. That information is as readily available to them as it is to the agent. It's irritating to have to go through all that when you book somebody.*

Jerry Kahn
Jerry Kahn, Inc.

• *I think mass mailings of pictures are a waste of time because they cost the actor hard-earned money. I think they should be sent out with discretion.*
My best advice is to get a job somewhere around the

business. *That way, you are going to get to know other actors and directors. If you are in a theater, agents are going to come in and see the showcase. If they aren't coming, someone in the show might call their agent and say,* Hey, see this person. He's really got something.

Lionel Larner
Lionel Larner Ltd.

• *Don't expose yourself to the agents and casting directors until you are really ready, because lots of people in the business have tunnel vision and will remember the one bad first audition.*

Gary Epstein
Epstein/Wyckoff

• *Get a good picture that accurately represents you at your best. There are some photographers that take the most gorgeous pictures in the world and they don't look a damn thing like what the kids look like. You really want an accurate representation of who you are. It better be a look that you can duplicate when you walk into an office.*

Flo Rothacker
DGRW

• *Get seen. Do something to be seen. Visibility is the name of the game. You're competing for the attention of the casting people. You've got to do something to make them aware of your existence.*

Jerry Kahn
Jerry Kahn, Inc.

• *The most important thing for an actor is continuity of management for an actor who wants to work all his life. Once you have established a reputation within the business that you are a good performer, the telephone generally rings. Your name is on a submission list. Yes, she's right*

for this. No, she's not right for that.
                                        Jerry Hogan
                                        Henderson/Hogan

Loose Lips Sink Ships

In World War II (the last time our citizens were patriotic), there was a real consciousness that information could be used against you. Fifty years have gone by, but the sentiment is still true. Regardless of how it lonely it may seem at times, the world is very small. The world of show business is even smaller; be circumspect with your comments about other peoples' work. You don't know who is listening or who is related to whom. Bonni Allen, who has now moved her office to Los Angeles underscores this truth:

• *Actors have to learn to keep their mouths shut except when they are on auditions. Never talk in elevators. Never talk in rooms where you don't know people. Never. The bottom line is,* Don't talk.
                                        Bonni Allen
                                        Bonni Allen

I found Beverly Anderson to be one of the most candid, entertaining and helpful agents in town. When I asked her for her best advice, she thought for a moment and said:

• *Be smart. Don't be naive. If you're not smart, it doesn't make any difference how much talent you have or how beautiful you are. You're dead. In all my experience of 29 years, all the people that I can sit here and say,* They made it *they did not make it because they were the most talented or the most beautiful or even the best organized or the most driven. They made it because they were basically extremely smart human beings. It has nothing to do with the best looks and the best talents, the best voice or the best tap dancing ability. It's being smart. Donna Mills is smart. Alan Alda is smart. Johnny Carson is smart. Barbara Walters is smart. They made it because they're smart, not because of talent. Talent is just automatic in this business.*

Who's to say that Barbra Streisand has the best voice in the world? I mean, let's face it, she sings well and has gorgeous styling and she makes a great sound, but who's to say if she has the best voice? I think the one ingredient that counts the most in this business is smarts. You could be talented and be sucked in by some agent who signs you up and never sends you out and you sit there for five years and say, Well, I thought they were going to get me a job. *Is that smart?* They promised they'd do a movie for me next year.

To be smart is the best thing. Talent is like a dime a dozen out the window.

Beverly Anderson

Beverly Anderson

We're back to Buckminster Fuller. Them that has gets; them that don't won't. It's all up to you and how smart you are. Whether you make positive choices; whether you choose to take a walk *literally* at the first sign of negative thinking; how well you know which one you are. You <u>will</u> have just what you want. Isn't that nice? It's all in *your* hands.

Wrap Up

Analyze
- ✓ how the business works
- ✓ who gets hired
- ✓ who hires and why
- ✓ what actor is getting your parts?

✓ what do they have that you don't have?
✓ your strengths
✓ your weaknesses

Important
✓ focus on the process not the goal
✓ study
✓ nourish your talent
✓ be organized
✓ acquire business skills
✓ be *smart*

Conglomerate/Star Level

I guess we've all heard the joke about the actor who killed four people, ran over a baby, bombed a building, ran across the street into the William Morris Agency, and was never seen again. It's the quintessential actor story about the wisdom of being signed by a big conglomerate agency.

It certainly *seems* like it would be nice to have the same agent as Clint Eastwood, Emma Thompson and Marisa Tomei. But, is it really a good choice for *you*?

The question is perplexing and research doesn't support a definitive answer. As in all other important decisions — who to marry, which doctor, lawyer, whether or not to have elective surgery, etc. — your decision must be based upon a combination of investigation and instinct.

Research does lead to the conclusion that the star agencies — CAA, ICM, William Morris, APA — all have more information and the best likelihood of getting you in for meetings, auditions, and ultimately jobs, *if they want to*.

A successful writer friend of mine told of her adventure at one of the large conglomerates. She was making about $150,000 a year and an employer owed her money. She

kept calling her agent asking him to pursue it. The agent
was becoming increasingly irritated with her calls. She
finally left when the agent said, *I really wish you were more
successful and made more money so I wouldn't have to keep
having these conversations with you.*

I know there are millions of $ to be made, but if $150,000
per year is not enough to get the attention of *the big guys*,
there are a lot of other agents who will take your calls and
treat you respectfully for a lot less.

What do casting directors think about star agencies?

I asked one casting director, *Who do you call first and why?*
and he answered, *CAA, ICM, William Morris,* and
mentioned the name of a one man office.[1] The casting
director went on to say that although he can cast everything
from the conglomerates, that he dare not skip this particular
office because *everyone* on the list was special and capable
of brilliance.

He went on to explain that although many prestigious
independent agents have important *hot* new actors, that the
process is like shopping for a suit. If you want the best
suit, you go to Bergdorf Goodman first. At Blooming-
dale's, you can also get a beautiful suit and expect to spend
a comparable amount of money, but Borgdorf not only has
a suit, it has cachet; the perception that it is *the* source for
the new and the unusual.

Casting directors tell me they prefer to deal with Brian
Riordan (J. Michael Bloom) and other distinguished
independent agents and that an actor would be crazy to

----

[1]That agent is now deceased.

leave a prestigious independent agent like Richard Astor for a conglomerate. One of the reasons they might prefer dealing with an independent agent is that the power of the corporate agencies (and their ability to withhold big stars) must make them very tough negotiators.

And then, there is the training process to consider. This procedure is so rigorous and humiliating that agents who have been through it are said to have a difficult time holding onto their humanity. An article in Buzz magazine entitled "Slaves of Wilshire Boulevard" talks about a young agent *wanna-be* who decided the price was too high.

• *[Susan] Sharp wound up exiting Triad after fifteen months,* It was a toss-up between being institutionalized and leaving *she says.* The type of people who survive are people who can stand enormous abuse. Not that they start off that way. You see people change. You see people start óut as relatively nice, and by the time they're out of the mail room and on a desk for a year, they're raging assholes.
  In fact, that sort of personal transformation may be precisely the point. After all, in an industry that esteems the values and manners of the proverbial schoolyard-bully, what else should an agent be but an asshole.

>   "Slaves of
>   Wilshire Boulevard"
>   Andy Marx
>   Buzz
>   November/December 1991

It makes sense to choose powerful client lists, information and stature, however when I met a well-known actress at a party, she didn't agree. The actress works mostly in film, but had recently been more doing theater - an activity not prized by most conglomerate agencies since relatively little money is involved. She was unhappy that none of her agents could be bothered to come see her performance.

- *It's too much trouble to keep up with all those agents. They won't all come see your work. Who needs it?*

Would she return to the big conglomerate if she got *hot?*

- *I was* hot *when I was at the smaller agency. My name was on everybody's list anyway, I didn't need to have a big office behind me. The only way I'd ever go back to a big agency is with a very strong manager. That way, the manager could call and keep up with all those agents. So, no, I don't think it's necessarily a better business decision to be at a large conglomerate.*

It's true that the conglomerates have more power and information, but do power and information compensate for lack of personal attention? The power of the large agencies comes from the having a list of *powerful stars* and those powerful stars get the attention of the buyers *and* the agents.

- *Those who control the scripts, the actors - the information - rule the world.*

> "Is This the Next
> Mike Ovitz?"
> Joanna Schneller
> <u>GQ</u>
> May 1992

When you have Arnold Schwarzenegger, Sharon Stone and Joe Eszterhas on your list you have the attention of the buyers. The Catch-22 is that if you are Arnold or Sharon, you don't need star agencies — because *you* are the power — and if you are not Arnold or Sharon, you are *filler.*

A big star was in the final stages of closing a deal on an important movie. Lo and behold, a bigger star at the same agency (who gets even *more* money) decided he was interested in the project. The original plans were immediately shelved and the bigger star did the movie. The agency made a better deal for *themselves*. They were not working for the star at all. An independent agent might do the same thing, but the chances are less likely that he will be representing you *and* your closest competitor.

• *The problem is that they're too big and they can't possibly function as effectively for an individual client as any number of not huge agencies. I don't see it, even for a star. I don't see the personal attention. To me, negotiation is easy. You keep saying no until you get what you want.*

> Kenneth Kaplan
> Innovative Artists

Kenneth gave me that quote when he was still an independent agent. Since then, he has worked at APA, and now he is at Innovative Artists, a bi-coastal agency with an important list of actors, writers, directors and below-the-line personnel. What does he say now?

• *Yeah. I know I said some things about conglomerate agencies in your last book. But, I have to admit that being able to work from the script instead of The Breakdown — which is really somebody else's interpretation of what the script is, plus access to directors and producers really does take a lot of frustration out of being an agent.*

> Kenneth Kaplan
> Innovative Artists

• *ICM can provide you with more messengers and more tickets to this and that. They have more people and more*

*money than we ever do, but we can care. We have the time
to give you insights. One reason we keep honing the list is
so that we can give in time what we can't give in money. I
believe I can do a first rate-job. Absolutely.*

Barry Douglas
DGRW

• *I can give as fine a representation as the biggest
agency in town if I'm enthusiastic about someone because it
means I'm on the phone calling casting people, and they
respond to my enthusiasm.*

Mary Sames
Sames & Rollnick

There are many prestigious independent agencies that have
had a shot at *the big time,* so to speak, and chose to go
back to a more intimate way of doing business.

One of my favorite agents has groomed several stars. As
those stars became more and more important and demanded
more and more time, the agent wasn't interested in assuming new responsibilities. I don't think he ever minded when
the actors went to WMA or ICM. It just wasn't the type of
service that the agent wanted to provide. Gene Parseghian
(WMA) confessed to me that there are days when he wishes
he still had a small office with three or four people and 20
clients, tops.

Sandy Bresler, a successful, distinguished Los Angeles
agent (whose list includes Jack Nicholson, Judd Hirsch and
Randy Quaid) left William Morris and started his own
office (which became The Artists Agency). When that got
too big for him, he left and started his own smaller office
again. Of course, he did take Nicholson, Hirsch, et al.
with him. That helped.

Conglomerates are not equipped to handle actors who are not making a lot of money. They are not interested in building careers. They take you while you're *hot* and they drop you when you're not.

A close friend of mine was on a soap opera for ten years while her conglomerate agent collected his 10%. When she was suddenly written out of the script, she went for *an entire year* without an audition before she finally wised up and left for an independent agency.

Get it While You're Young, You're Aging Even as You Read

Star agencies are more interested in youth, not only because of the longevity factor, but because the most lucrative jobs in television and film (the leads) are for young good looking actors.

An actor usually needs the help of an independent agent or manager to get to a position to catch the eye of powerful agencies, but if you do, they *can* change your life. Julia Roberts' career is a good example. She came to New York in 1985 with a famous older brother (Eric) already working in the business. Through showbiz friends, she hooked up with manager Bob McGowan.

• *To get Roberts a role in "Satisfaction," a movie about an all-girl rock band, he lied:* Julia is a musician, *he informed the casting director - and enrolled her in a crash course in the drums* the easiest instrument to learn, *Roberts got the part. When McGowan offered the prestigious William Morris Agency 10% of the deal, it agreed to sign her up.*
Roberts was assigned to agent Risa Shapiro and Elaine Goldsmith in the company's West Coast office who joined

125

McGowan in guiding her career. The threesome lined up an episode of TV's "Crime Story" and a part in the HBO movie "Baja Oklahoma."

> "The Power of Julia"
> Elaine Dutka
> The Los Angeles Times
> June 9, 1991

Now Shapiro, Goldsmith and Roberts have moved to ICM and Julia has dumped McGowan.

• *...Roberts left McGowan, her manager, without explanation. She hasn't hired another.* That was the first completely difficult decision I had to make in my life, *she says.* Bob had gone to bat for me, but I felt I had to be honest. We'd outgrown each other. There were too many people around me making decisions and I wanted a clearer line between me and the work.

> "The Power of Julia"
> Elaine Dutka
> Los Angeles Times
> June 9, 1991

Conglomerate agencies have served Roberts well, but Debra Winger had a different experience,

• *"Legal Eagles" was a packaged movie. In other words, the powerful Creative Artists Agency (CAA) representing the actors (Robert Redford and Debra Winger), the director, Ivan Reitman, and other key participants, had brought the tied-up bundle to Universal Pictures and taking its commissions, walked off with a bundle in return.* I'll never do another film like that, *says Winger. The experience confirmed her doubts about the agency system.* There's nothing creative about being packaged, *she says.* You're just being used. Before, if you had an agent and you were at a point in your career when you weren't happy, your agent might suggest, *Well, you know, there's this little movie or this little play and there's no money, but you might find it interesting. Now, they would never do that.*

"Debra Wings It"
Arthur Lubow
<u>Vanity Fair</u>
February, 1987

Since that article, Winger left CAA, worked through her lawyer for a while and has since returned to CAA.

ICM, WMA and CAA inadvertently gave me great insight into the complexity of their operations when I asked for interviews and the history of their agencies. Completely unavailable for any kind of interview, their legal departments all ended up referring me to the *popular press* as they termed it.

A few hours at the Academy of Motion Picture Arts and Sciences Library brought me much more interesting information than might have been offered by company spokespeople. From the <u>Daily Variety Forty-Sixth Anniversary Issue</u>:

• If I told you how many people I represented, *admitted a senior v.p. at one of the major agencies in town,* I'd immediately get a call from five other people I represented the next day saying, "How much time can you spend on me when you're worrying about everybody else. No wonder I'm not getting work."

An agent's primary responsibility is supposed to be guiding and building a career for his client. That's the belief of everyone from the president of William Morris to an agent who handles under 25 people. But a number of observers express concern that the large agencies have essentially become bookers of talent *that do little more than service the marketplace with a particular set of goods.*

One veteran staffer at ICM who recently left the fold to become a manager said he found himself in a position where, There was no way I could devote the real amount of attention needed to all of my clients. There were just too many. *The head of a small agency in town related that he'd heard the William Morris Agency did work through computer printouts of their actors and that if a client's name began with anything under an L, he was at a distinct disadvantage.*

> "The Agents: Poobahs of Power and Price"
> Steven Ginsberg
> <u>Daily Variety</u>
> October 30, 1979

• *More powerful than Sylvester Stallone, Steven Spielberg or Barry Diller, the most influential person in Hollywood is not a star, a director or a studio head. While his name is rarely in the news media and he never gets a screen credit, everyone who matters in the industry knows who he is. He is assiduously courted by producers and studio heads alike because they need his cooperation in order to gain the services of the best writers, stars and directors in the industry. He is Mike Ovitz, the president of Creative Artists Agency (CAA).*

CAA does not have the bureaucracy of William Morris or the bickering of ICM. It has restrained its growth and carefully chosen its agents with an eye toward their ability to work well together. CAA partner Martin Baum says his agency is successful because its agents put the welfare of the agency ahead of their own interests. The policy of this company from its inception has been that we all profit if one succeeds. *It has been the first time that there has been a total sublimation of the individual ego for the betterment of the group.*

Reel Power
Mark Litwak
William Morrow & Co.

I heartily recommend <u>Reel Power</u> for insights into the motion picture business in all areas, most particularly what Mark Litwak has to say about actors and agents.

In 1990, there was an enormous shifting of power among the star agencies, CAA became even more powerful when Mike Ovitz (besides representing seemingly all the *big players* in the motion picture business [Cher, Sean Connery, Tom Cruise, Danny De Vito, etc.]) acted as the power broker in the buyout of Universal Films by the Japanese company, Matsushita.

Another agency upset was detailed in the August 1991 issue of <u>Premiere</u> Magazine.

● *It didn't sound like big news at first - just a terse announcement in the trades that senior William Morris agent Toni Howard had ankled her post for International Creative Management, taking with her such star clients as Anjelica Huston, James Spader, and Jason Robards. But a week later, when Elaine Goldsmith and Risa Shapiro joined her, taking Julia Roberts, Tim Robbins, and Andie MacDowell, it began to look serious.*

"The Case of the
Ankling Agents"
Frank Rose
<u>Premiere Magazine</u>
August 1991

Get a copy of <u>Premiere</u> and read the whole story. It is fascinating. Suffice to say that ICM now has a much more even standing with CAA in the quantity and quality of their stars.

In 1992, Triad merged with William Morris and Los Angeles' prestigious InterTalent closed its doors. Their powerful agents and clients moved to ICM and United Talent (for the most part) enlarging the power bases of those agencies.

Although CAA's Mike Ovitz appears to be the most powerful agent, there are those who think Sam Cohn at ICM is certainly his equal though Cohn did lose Meryl Streep to CAA in 1992.

Following behind CAA and ICM are William Morris, United Talent and APA. You'd probably be thrilled to be in the company of the names on any of their lists. The casting people do say they call them first, mainly because the casting director is looking for a star to front a project. But Robert Lantz, Clifford Stevens, Lionel Larner, Martin Gage, Richard Astor, Bret Adams, and many other independent agents also have star clients.

It's awesome standing in the library of APA in Los Angeles. More scripts than I have read in my lifetime (and I've read a lot) are all standing cover sheet to cover sheet begging for attention. These are scripts that are somewhere on the development path. All those APA agents have access to the information and they have that access before the package is even completed. They could tell you today to lose 25 pounds for a part because the part is a year away. And APA doesn't even refer to itself as a conglomerate, they say they are *mid-sized*.

When all is said and done, the swell offices, script libraries, limos, flowers, and packaging considered, you'll make your decision based on what is important to you. Do you want a family member or do you want a corporation?

My vote would be for the prestigious, successful, tasteful mid-level agency. Of course, no one has plied me with limos and flowers yet either.

Wrap Up

Conglomerates
- ✓ have more information
- ✓ command more power
- ✓ have access to more perks
- ✓ can package effectively
- ✓ give less personal attention
- ✓ advice is corporate
- ✓ lose interest when you are not in demand

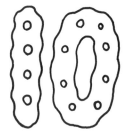

Managers/Packaging/Etc.

My experience with managers doesn't lead me to recommend them, however, I *have* spoken to a few actors who felt the presence of a manager enhanced their careers. A Los Angeles actress friend was able to work closely enough with her manager to keep her career going until she could interest an agent. The actress and the manager, who had access to the Breakdown, were able to go over the Breakdown together to determine appropriate projects. The actress then dropped off the submission at the studio announcing that it was a delivery from *Miss Whoever*. The casting director then booked her directly. Although more helpful than not being represented, this only worked up to a point, because the manager didn't have that much access on her own.

Under any kind of normal circumstances, it seems odd to me that someone would want to spend a minimum of 15% of their income to get the service we all hope to get from our agent, but there are a few situations in which I can see a manager being helpful:

☞ If you are entering the business and need someone to help you decide about pictures, resumes, how to dress, etc. The Julia Roberts story is a good example. The manager got her started, but at a later point, she decided she no longer needed that kind of service. There are, however, many agents who pride themselves on getting young actors started and offering that kind of support.

☞ If you are at a big agency and it's too intimidating and time-consuming to call and keep in touch with many agents.

☞ Some actors find changing agents more helpful when they have access to a managers contacts. The manager makes the calls, sets things up and cushions you and the agents from rejection. It's a pretty expensive way to get an agent. If you've got the credits to support getting a good agent, you could do it on your own. And if you don't, the manager can't create them.

Packaging

A large agency representing writers, directors, producers and actors has a script written by one of its writers. The script has a great part for one of its stars or first-billed actors. It then selects one of its directors and calls CBS or Paramount or whomever and says, *Star writer has just written a terrific script for our star actress and our star director is interested. Are you?*

CBS says, *Yes*, and a package is sold. Television pilots, TV movies, theatrical films, etc., are all participants in this process called packaging on one level or another. Non-star actors frequently choose agencies with package potential because they feel they, too, will get jobs out of the arrangement.

In the interests of its members, Screen Actors Guild commissioned its own study regarding packaging. The study reviewed seven packaged TV series, three packaged miniseries and two packaged feature films. It found only 27 of the 372 roles created for these packaged projects went to actors who were represented by agents doing the packaging or slightly more than two roles per project.

• *You maybe can put the first-billed actor, maybe the second actor, but at that point people at the studios and the networks want their creative input.*

John Kimble
William Morris Agency

Pictures

There are many good photographers in town. Some are better than others. A handful take the major portion of actor pictures. Here is a list of photographers who are well thought of in town. Don't just choose one off the list. Make an appointment to go by and meet the photographer and look at his book. Meet at least three before deciding. See who you feel most comfortable with and whose look appeals to you the most. Look through The Players Guide and begin to notice what makes you look at one picture more than another. Look at the pictures your friends are using and find out about their photographers. Prices vary from $175 to $500 and more. An expensive price tag doesn't guarantee a better picture. It's possible to get the perfect picture for under $200. The bottom line is *make sure the picture looks like you.*

Photographers

David Brown	Suzanne Gold
Andrew Bruckner	Manning Gurney
Ginsey Dauk	Joe Henson

Glen Jussin   Mark Robay (pretty)
Ralph Lewin   Tess Steinkolk (essence)
David Morgan (men)   Joan Vincent
              Van Williams (natural)

Resume

Your 8x10 glossy print is sent with your resume. You can
have your picture printed with or without a white border
(some agents prefer the picture without border, but it is
usually more expensive). The resume should be stapled to
the back so that as you turn the picture over, you see the
resume as though it were printed on the back side of the
photo. The buyers see hundreds of resumes every day.
Yours should be simple and easy to read. Not only is it not
necessary to have millions of jobs listed, but when
prospective employers see too much writing, their eyes will
glaze over and they won't read anything. Choose the most
impressive credits and list them. There is an example on
the next page to use as a guide for form. You may have
nothing to put on your resume. If that's true, at least list
your training and a physical description. Lead with your
strong suit. If you have done more commercials than
anything else, list that as your first category; if you are a
singer, list *music*. You may live in a market where theater
credits are taken very seriously. If this is so, even though
you may have done more commercials, lead with theater if
you have anything credible to report.

Adapt this example to meet your needs. If all you have
done is college theater, list it. What you have done is
more than someone else has done and it will give the buyer
an idea of what you can do. Note that you were master of
ceremonies for your town Pioneer Day Celebration. If you
sing, list where. Accomplishments that might seem trivial
to you could be important to someone else, particularly if

Mary Smith\212-555-4489
5'4", 115 lbs, Blonde hair, blue eyes

Theater

Hamlet . . . . name of theater
Lost in Yonkers . . . . name of theater

Film

Tootsie . . . . name of director
Soapdish . . . . name of director

Television

Who's the Boss? . . . . name of director
LA Law . . . . name of director

Commercials

First National Bank, Local Gas Company, Local
Newspaper, etc.

Training

acting . . . . teacher
singing . . . . teacher
dance . . . . teacher

Skills: Speak Spanish fluently, horseback riding,
gymnastics, ballroom dancing, commercial driving
license, etc.

you phrase it right. As you have more important credits, drop the less impressive ones.

My own opinion is not to put your union affiliation (Screen Actors Guild, Actors Equity Association, American Federation of Television and Radio Artists) on the resume. As far I am concerned, if you list them, you are making a big deal of it. If you are a member of the unions, of course you are. If you are not that far along yet, don't bring it to their attention.

The most important thing on your resume is your name and *service* phone number *or* your agents' name and number prominently displayed. Don't use your personal phone number on resumes. There are a lot of weird people out there. It's safer and more professional to list your representation, service or phone mail.

Top of the Show

This is a phrase heard much more in Los Angeles than in New York and refers to wages paid to *guest* in television episodes. Years ago guest stars routinely received $10,000 or more per week. Then, in 1961, television reruns became subject to residual payments to actors. Soon after producers got together and decided to stop negotiating with actors playing guest leads in television episodes and set a predetermined cap for appearances on half-hour and hour shows.

It's actually *restraint of trade* for anyone to *price fix* so during this time all the buyers acted as though they had never heard the term they routinely used when booking actors. The exalted *top of the show* fee that casting directors and producers bandied about was *less* than a minimum day fee multiplied by the number of days worked, due to an unfortunate prior contract that called for *discounts* allowed for multiple days worked.

Screen Actors Guild has finally been able to address *TOS* in contract negotiations. It's still not a great rate, but it's better than it was and the discount for multiple days has been eliminated. The official term is now *major role*.

When I worked in California in 1976, *top of the show* was $1,000 for a half-hour and $1,500 for an hour. Today, top for a half-hour is $1,864 and $3,262 for an hour show. This new designation of payment requires the actor be hired in what is called the guest-star category and credits are shown *before* the show or on a separate card at the end.

If you are not in a position to negotiate for at least *top of the show*, minimum for a day on a television show is $466. There's nothing wrong with working for minimum if that is where your rate is, but management, by attaching the *TOS/MR* designation, implies the actor is getting some kind of preferred rate, when mostly it's not that much more than minimum for a day times the number of days. Actors with high visibility still routinely command $15,000 for a guest appearance on a one-hour show.

There are a few shows, notably those produced by Aaron Spelling that routinely break the top or have no top. They also routinely hire stars whose fees are far above TOS, so Mr. Spelling's generosity rarely benefits the working actor.

The Breakdown Service

The Breakdown Service originated in Los Angeles. Years ago agents drove to each studio every day, read each script, made their submissions and repeated the process at the next studio. Finally, an enterprising chap named Gary Marsh (who was having to read all the scripts anyway for his mother, who was an agent) called the studios and said something like:

- *I think I could make your life better. If you give me all your scripts, I will summarize them and make a list of the types of actors needed for the parts, the size of each role, etc., and provide that information to all the agents. This will save you the nuisance of having all those people there and them the inconvenience of driving.*

The venerable Breakdown Service was born. It costs the agents a hefty amount to subscribe, but is well worth it. When agents subscribe to the service, they must agree not to show it to actors. This makes some actors angry and they make litigious noises and scream *restraint of trade*, although the reality of sharing this information with every actor would grind the business to a halt in about 15 minutes. There are enough agents scrambling to get *their* submissions to casting directors, that if actors were all sending their pictures with no screening process, casting directors would have to dump all submissions, not just those of *unconnected* agents and managers. Some actors do get hold of the Breakdown. Some use the information intelligently and others merely alienate their agents with it.

Although the Breakdown is invaluable, it doesn't include everything. Many episodic parts are filled by casting directors who just call and ask for the actors they want to see, this saves everyone's time, cutting down on *cattle call* casting, but makes it more difficult for actors who are not already established to be seen. Many features don't come out in Breakdown unless the casting director has an unusual role to fill. Casting directors have extensive files of their own culled from years in the business and usually exhaust those resources before calling on The Breakdown Service.

Since not everything comes out in Breakdown, it is important to attempt to assess the other contacts your agent has in addition to the Breakdown. If your agent is not in a position to have more information than is in the Breakdown, that's still a lot of information, if he uses it wisely.

Your Reference Library

When I was still living in New York, I was fortunate enough to get a part in what turned out to be a very important film, "A Touch of Class," which was shot in Spain. The night after I arrived in Marbella, there was a cocktail party in honor of the cast. I found myself standing next to the wife of the writer-producer-director:

Oh, I said to Mel Frank's wife, *what a wonderful script. Is this Mel's first script?* Sweet, kind, tolerant Ann Frank then enumerated her husband's incomparable credits. A Hollywood legend, a few of Mel's credits include "White Christmas", "A Funny Thing Happened on the Way to the Forum", and "Mr. Blandings Builds His Dreamhouse."

Fortunately, I had the grace to apologize for my ignorance and confess embarrassment and Ann couldn't have been sweeter saying, *This will be our little secret.* I vowed then and there to educate myself about all potential collaborators.

I now own many books that have the credits of writers, directors, and producers and consider my research library an invaluable part of my business. Just as a producer or director wants to know your resume before he sees you, you will benefit from having that information on your auditioners as well as biographies of successful people who will provide role models in your quest for achievement.

Books about writing and directing should also be part of

your collection and publications that list credits are indispensable. The Directors Guild of America — Directory of Members and The Writers Guild Membership Directory are invaluable. Inexpensive and available to non-members, they list names, credits and representation of members. If you cannot find these books at a theater book store, you can order through the respective guilds.

Writers Guild/East   Directors Guild of America
555 West 57th Street   110 West 57th Street
New York, NY 10019   New York, NY 10019

Another important book is casting by..., a directory of the Casting Society of America, its members and their credits. This is available at Drama Books or order direct from:

Breakdown Services
1120 South Robertson Blvd., 3rd Floor
Los Angeles, CA 90035

Many actors are not aware there are such books and that they are available to anyone who wants to buy them.

Ask your agent to save his old copy of The Players Guide for you when he gets his new one. This is a handy reference guide when you want to check out just who it was who got your part.

Biographies of actors are instructive and inspirational. When you read Desi Arnaz' A Book, detailing his escape from Cuba with his father and how resourceful they had to be to survive, it's easy to understand how he pioneered a whole new concept in television. His story more than supports the concept that courage, vision and persistence are as important as talent and training.

Carol Burnett's biography, <u>One More Time</u> makes you believe that *anything* really can happen. Nobody ever had more bad luck than Charles Grodin who talks about in <u>It Would Be So Nice If You Weren't Here</u>. Tony Randall's book, <u>Which Reminds Me</u> has more funny stories about life in the theater than you'll ever be able to remember, but they will cheer you when life seems bleak.

Books like <u>Wired</u>, <u>Indecent Exposure</u>, and <u>Saturday Night Live</u> serve to remind of the pitfalls of sudden success and the peril of losing one's value system. It's easy to get caught up in the glamour of publicity, money and power.

Recently it was my pleasure to attend the opening of a play written by Jonathan Tolins, who was the stage manager on a play I appeared in a few years ago at The Matrix Theater in Los Angeles. A year later, he produced his own first play. Today, his second play, "Twilight of the Golds" is having a major production and has been sold to films. He's only four years out of college and his name is all over the trades. Important people are vying for his attention, but he still has enough perspective to check himself about getting *too big for my britches*, as he put it.

It's difficult to remember you are a mere mortal when others tell you you're God, so give yourself a break and have supportive reading by your bedside at all times.

I cannot stress strongly enough the need for a good reference library. I'm including a list of books that will give your library a good start. If you know of any books that belong on this list, please advise me and I'll include them in subsequent editions.

Beginning Reference Library

A Book/Desi Arnaz
Adventures in the Screen Trade/William Goldman
AFTRA Agency Regulations
A Passion for Acting/Alan Miller
Audition/Michael Shurtleff
The Complete Directory to Primetime Network
    TV Shows/Tim Brooks-Earle Marsh
Equity Agency Regulations
The Film Encyclopedia/Ephraim Katz
The Filmgoer's Companion/Leslie Halliwell
Final Cut/Steven Bach
Halliwell's Film Guide/Leslie Halliwell
How to Sell Yourself as an Actor/K Callan
Indecent Exposure/David McClintock
The LA Agent Book/K Callan
NY Times Directory of Film/(Arno Press)
NY Times Directory of Theatre/(Arno Press)
Reel Power/Mark Litwak
Ross Reports Television/(Television Index)
Saturday Night Live/Doug Hall-Jeff Weingrad
Screen Actors Guild Agency Regulations
Screen World/current edition John Willis
The Season/William Goldman
Theatre World/current edition John Willis
You'll Never Have Lunch in this
    Town Again/Julia Phillips
TV Movies/Leonard Maltin
Who's Who in the Motion Picture Industry
    /Rodman Gregg
Who's Who in American Film Now/James Monaco
Wired/Bob Woodward

Wrap Up

Have a business overview
- ✓ packaging
- ✓ breakdown
- ✓ top of the show

Keep Informed
- ✓ reference library

Professional Tools
- ✓ pictures
- ✓ resumes

Glossary

The Academy Players Directory — Los Angeles version of The Players Guide. Annual catalogue of actors showing one or two pictures per actor, credits and representation. You must have a franchised agent or be a member of one of the performers' unions to be listed. Casting directors, producers and others who routinely track actors use the book as a reference guide. Every actor who is *ready to book* should be in this directory.

Actor's unions:

Actors Equity Association — Equity covers actors' employment in the theatre.

American Federation of Television and Radio Artists — AFTRA covers actors employed in videotape and radio.

Screen Actors Guild — SAG covers actors employed in theatrical motion pictures and all product for *filmed* television including informercials and music Videos.

Answering Services — Answering services come in many forms. The most expensive ones have a tie-in to your phone at home and after a predesignated number of rings they will pick up your line. Usually they announce themselves with your phone number or name and note messages you receive. Less expensive services have a central number you give to business contacts and you call in for your messages. The alternative is a good answering machine. Get one or the other the minute you hit town; actors simply cannot function without reliable telephone support. Some really paranoid actors (me, for one) have a machine and a service for when the machine is broken or the phone is out. I have had Actorfone for almost 20 years and love them, but there are any number of reputable answering services that exclusively represent actors. Check Dramalogue for ads or ask friends about their services.

Audition tape — Also known as a Composite Cassette Tape. A videotape usually no longer than ten minutes, showcasing either one performance or a montage of scenes of an actor's work. Most agents and casting directors prefer to see tapes of professional appearances only (film or television), but some will look at a tape produced for audition purposes.

Breakdown Service — Started in 1971 in Los Angeles by Gary Marsh, the Service condenses scripts and lists parts available in films, television, and theatre. Expensive and available to agents and managers only.

Clear — When actors work on a free-lance basis, the unions demand that the agent check with the actor (clearing) before submitting him on a particular project.

Composite Cassette Tape — See Audition tape.

Equity Waiver — See Showcases.

Free-lance — Term used to describe the relationship between an actor and agent or agents who submit the actor for work without an exclusive contract. New York agents frequently will work on this basis, Los Angeles agents rarely consent to this arrangement.

Going out — Auditions or meetings with directors and/or casting directors. Usually set up by your agent but have also been set up by very persistent and hardy actors.

The Leagues — A now defunct formal collective of prestigious theatre schools that offer conservatory training for the actor. The schools still exist, but there is no longer an association. The best background an actor can have, as far as agents are concerned other than having your father own a studio. They are American Conservatory Theatre in San Francisco, CA; American Repertory Theatre, Harvard University in Cambridge, MA; Boston University in Boston, MA; Carnegie Mellon in Pittsburgh, PA; Catholic University in Washington, DC; The Julliard School in New York City, NY; New York University in New York City, NY; North Carolina School of the Arts in Winston Salem, NC; Southern Methodist University in Dallas, TX; The University of CA at San Diego in La Jolla, CA and the Yale Drama School in New Haven, CT.

Letter of Termination — A legal document dissolving the contract between actor and agent. If you decide to leave your agent while your current contract is in effect, it is usually possible to do so citing Paragraph 6 of the SAG Agency Regulations. Paragraph 6 allows either the actor or the agent to terminate the contract if the actor has not worked for more than 15 of the previous 91 days by sending a letter of termination.

Dear :
This is to inform you that relative to Paragraph 6 of the Screen Actors Basic Contract, I am terminating our contract as of ___ date.

Send a copy of the letter to your agent via registered mail, return receipt requested, plus copies to the Screen Actors Guild and all unions involved. Retain a copy for your files.

Membership Requirements for Unions:

AFTRA — Membership requirements are pretty lenient and seem to be based on having the money to pay the enrollment fee. Note: It can be a hindrance to join unions before you are ready as that puts you out of the running to do non-union films, shows, etc., and amass film on yourself. AFTRA's initiation fee is $800. Dues are payable semiannually and are based on the performer's gross earnings under AFTRA's jurisdiction for the previous year. The lowest amount of annual dues (on earnings up to $2,000) is $84. If you make over $100,000, you pay $1,000.

Equity — Rules for membership state you must have a verifiable Equity Contract in order to join or have been a member in good standing for at least one year in AFTRA or SAG. Initiation fee is currently $800, payable prior to election to membership. Basic dues are $37 twice a year. Additionally, there are working dues: 2% of gross weekly earnings from employment. This 2% is deducted from your check before you receive it in the same way your income tax is deducted.

SAG — The most sought after union card. Actors may join SAG upon proof of employment or prospective employment within two weeks or less by a SAG signatory film, television program or commercial.

Proof of employment may be in the form of a signed contract, a payroll check or check stub, or a letter from the company (on company letterhead stationery). The document proving employment must state the applicant's name, Social Security number, the name of the production or commercial, the salary paid in dollar amount and the dates worked. Another way of joining SAG is by being a paid up member of an affiliated performers' union for a period of at least one year and have worked at least once as a principal performer in that union's jurisdiction.

SAG's initiation fee is $974.50 This seems like a lot of money (and is) but the formula involved makes some sense. It is SAG minimum ($466) for two days work ($932) plus the first semiannual dues ($42.50). This money is payable in full, in cashier's check or money order, at the time of application. The fees may be lower in some branch areas. SAG dues are based on SAG earnings and are billed twice a year. Those members earning more than $5,000 annually under SAG contracts will pay 1½% of all money earned in excess of $5,000 up to a maximum of $150,000.

Minimums — for the most accurate up-to-date numbers, call your union and ask them to send you a book listing all the contracts and pay scales.

Actors Equity Association — There are 18 basic contracts ranging from the low end of the Small Production Contract (from $125 to $390 weekly depending on the size of the theatre) to the higher Production Contract (covering Broadway houses, Jones Beach, etc. $925 weekly). Highest is the Industrial Contract, for shows produced by large corporations ($1,088 for first week or $870 each week in a multiple week contract).

American Federation of Television and Radio Artists — The minimum for one day on a television show for network/primetime is the same as for SAG — $466. Fox is not considered network nor is syndication. For taped syndicated shows other than commercials, the fee is $458 for 10½ hours over a two day period. That means they can call you at any time over a 48 hour period and have you work 2 hours and then come back in 4 hours and work for 30 minutes until the job is finished or the ten half hours are used up. Then they go into overtime. The half hours do not have to be consecutive. Wonder why AFTRA is an unpopular union?   414.25 a day for a commercial on camera and $311.50 for a 2 hour session for a voice over.

Night-time rates for primetime are on a parity with Screen Actors Guild (see their rates). Day rates for soap operas are $422 for a principal role on a half hour show (based on a 9 hour workday) and $563 for a one hour show. There is also a category for performers who speak five lines or less (frequently referred to as *five or under*). It pays $200 for a half hour show and $246 for an hour show.

There are special categories and different fees for announcers, newscasters, singers, chorus, etc., as well as radio and voice over. The fees I am quoting are for straight on camera acting.

Screen Actors Guild — Scale rates require $466 daily and $2,330 weekly as a minimum for employment in films and television. Overtime in SAG is considerably higher than in AFTRA.

Overexposed — Term used by nervous buyers (producers, networks, casting directors, etc.) indicating an actor has become too recognizable for their tastes. Maybe he just got off a situation comedy and everyone remembers him as a particular character. The buyer doesn't want the public thinking of that instead of his project. A thin line exists between not being recognizable and being overexposed.

Packaging — Practice involves a talent agency approaching a buyer with material (writer), a star, usually a star director and possibly a producer already attached to it. May include any number of other writers, actors, producers, etc.

Paid Auditions — There is no formal name for the practice of rounding up 20 actors and charging them $10 each for the *privilege* of meeting a casting director, agent, producer, etc. There are agents, casting directors, and actors who feel the practice is unethical. It does give some actors who would otherwise not be seen an opportunity to meet and be seen by casting directors. I feel that meeting a casting director under these circumstances is questionable and that there are more productive ways to spend your money.

Per Diem — Negotiated amount of money for expenses on location or on the road *per day*.

Pictures — The actor's calling card. An 8x10 glossy black and white photograph.

Pilot — The first episode of a proposed television series. Produced so that the network can determine whether there will be additional episodes. There are many pilots made every year. Few go to series. Fewer stay on the air for more than a single season.

Players Guide — Catalogue of actors published annually for the New York market. Shows one or two pictures per actor and lists credits and representation. If you work free-lance, you can list your name and service. Some list union affiliation. Casting directors, producers, and whoever else routinely keeps track of actors use the book as a reference guide. Every actor who is ready to book should be in this catalogue. Los Angeles counterpart is The Academy Players Directory.

Ready to Book — Agent talk for an actor who has been trained and judged mature enough to handle himself well in the audition, not only with material, but also with the buyers. Frequently refers to an actor whose progress in acting class or theater has been monitored by the agent.

Resumes — The actor's ID; lists credits, physical description, agent's name, and phone contact.

Right — When someone describes an actor as being *right* for a part, he is speaking about the essence of an actor. We all associate a particular essence with Paul Newman and a difference essence with Woody Allen. One would not expect Woody Allen and Paul Newman to be up for the same part. Being *right* also involves credits. The more important the part, the more credits are necessary to support being seen.

Rollcall — Like The Players Guide except information is fed into subscribers' computers. The advantage is you can update your resume as often as you like. Lots of differing opinions on this. Some agents think it's stupid. I don't see the harm. It doesn't cost that much to be listed and many important buyers subscribe.

Scale — See minimums.

Showcases — Productions in which members of Actors Equity are allowed by the union to work without compensation are called Showcases in New York and Equity Waiver or Waiver Productions in Los Angeles. Equity members are allowed to perform as long as the productions conform to certain Equity guidelines: rehearsal conditions, limiting the number of performances and seats, providing a set number of complimentary tickets for cast members, etc. If you do a Showcase, do yourself a favor and stop by Equity to get a copy of your rights. Very interesting.

Sides — The pages of script containing your audition material. Usually not enough information to use as a source to do a good audition. If they won't give you a complete script, go early (or the day before), sit in the office, and read it. SAG rules require producers to allow actors access to the script (if it's written).

Submissions — Agent talk for the act of sending an actor's name to a casting director in hopes of getting the actor an audition or meeting for a part.

Talent — Industry wide term used to describe an actor or actors.

Top of the Show — A predetermined fee set by producers which is a non-negotiable maximum for guest appearances on television episodes. Aka *major role*. See minimums.

The Trades — <u>Backstage</u> and <u>Showbusiness</u> cover all kinds of show business news, including classes, auditions and castings and are particularly helpful to newcomers. Los Angeles counterpart is <u>Dramalogue</u>. Los Angeles daily trades <u>Variety</u> and <u>Hollywood Reporter</u> include more on film and television and showbiz financial news. All are available at good newsstands or by subscription.

Under Five — An AFTRA job in which the actor has five or fewer lines. Paid at a specific rate. Less than a principal and more than an extra.

Visible/Visibility — Currently on view in film, theatre or television. In this business, it's *out of sight, out of mind* so visibility is very important.

Rating the Agents

Actors frequently write asking that I rate agents in some way. When I first contemplated writing this book, I guess I thought it might be like a restaurant guide, with five ★ agents, four ★, etc., but it turns out that agents and agencies are not at all like chefs and restaurants. You can't rate them with ★'s or even with $'s (though that might be more accurate).

A more accurate way to group agents considers size and experience: star agency conglomerates, boutique star agencies, prestigious working-actor agencies as well evolving agents building their business who will clearly have status as their client list matures. The rankings involve access, stature and size; there are about six levels.

Use all the resources of this book in making your decision: the client list, the agents' own words *and* the listing of each agency. I have provided statistics and tried to characterize each agency. If I don't mention client names at the end of a listing, that was the agent's request either because he felt it was an invasion of client privacy, was afraid of another agent stealing the clients or had no one to point to. When you check the list at SAG, you'll be able to make your own determination.

The Los Angeles Times, November 15, 1987 ran an article,

"The Glut of Actors - Enough Already!" by Lawrence
Christon which though generally negative, did say,

- *Success in the entertainment industry, particularly that
portion that uses actors, involves enough paradoxes and
variables to prevent anyone from telling anyone else that
he/she doesn't have a chance.*

He could as easily have been writing about agents; it's
unwise to write anyone off. So much about show business
is perception.

As Bret Adams put it,

- *There are agents who are good guys and agents who
are lousy guys. There are actors who are good guys and
there are actors who are bad guys. It's an individual thing.
I don't buy that an actor doesn't know that.*

When I interviewed agents, they were usually on their best
behavior — as they would be with you if they were wooing
you. Reality emerges over time not on first meetings,
that's why God invented dating. Most New York agents
mentioned that they prefer to get to know clients on a brief
free-lance basis before signing. That way everyone gets a
more accurate picture of the possibilities.

Deciding which agents to include in my book is always a
challenge. Should I include anybody who will talk to me?
Only those agents that I could actually in good conscience
recommend? It seems inappropriate for me to try to play
God about who is worthy and who is not. On the other
hand, I don't want my readers to think I would recommend
everyone who is in the book. That automatically makes
anyone *not* in the book suspect.

And there are people who for whatever reason won't talk to
me. And I'm not referring to Mike Ovitz. I didn't even

try to call Mr. Ovitz. What am I going to ask someone like Mike Ovitz? *Gee, tell me, Mike, what's the best way for Meryl Streep to talk to you if she's not working?*

Shall I ask him the best way to keep in touch with him, if I am his client? I have no idea what it is like to exist in that area of the business. I am confident, however, that someone reading this book right now has embarked on a journey that will take him/her to that level of the business. And if I am helpful to you in any way, I'll be expecting a call from you when you get there to fill me in on this particular information.

Shall I leave out everyone who has a chip on his shoulder? And how could I tell? Maybe I caught him on a bad day, or some real bad guy on his best day? How can I in good conscience not tell you when an agent tells me something that I know to be untrue. If an agent tells me he has *many clients on series and in films,* but declines to name them, it does make me suspicious. All I have to do is travel to SAG to check the client lists to find out if my suspicions are correct. And I always check. You should, too. If the agent is misrepresenting the facts, no need to confront him, just cross him off your list. I did.

There are some people who have been in business for years, who don't really *represent* their talent. They just send in lots of pictures. Many casting directors don't even open these agents' submissions. Some agents talk a better game than they play. Remember, it is better to have no agent than an agent who is going to lie to you.

Movies and disgruntled actors perpetuate certain agent stereotypes: *They lie, that's their job.* I imagine about the same percentage of agents lie as do actors. It depends on the person. Most agents are hard working, professional regular people who, *like actors* want to make it in show business. They too, want to be respected for their work, go to the Academy Awards and get great tables at Sardi's. And they, like actors, are willing to put up with the toughest, most humiliating, most heartbreaking business in the world because they are mavericks who love the adventure and can't think of a single thing that interests them more than show business.

I'm listing all the agents I interviewed. If I didn't interview yours, it's either because I didn't get around to him, he wouldn't talk to me or I didn't know about him. Most of the time, I went to the office because that was more convenient for the agent and also, that information helped me make judgements about the agent. A couple of times, at the agent's suggestion, we met at a restaurant. I suspect it was because the agent didn't want me to see the office. I didn't meet everyone in the agency or all the partners, but I did meet with a partner or an agent, who was acting as a spokesman for the company. I could be wrong in my judgments, but at least they are not based on hearsay.

Because the business has been in such a state of flux and recession for the past few years, many agencies have closed or merged with others under new names. For this reason, when you decide to write a letter to an agent, double check the address by the most current edition of The Ross Reports or by calling to verify the current address.

Agents reflect the business. If you are employed in the business in any visible way, people are usually nice to you and validate your existence. If you are not, the lack of respect is chilling. Keep your wits and your sense of humor about you and you'll gain perspective when the same people fawn over you once you actually do some visible work. I'm sure that I'm the same individual when I'm out of work as I am when I am working. I don't think I become smarter, prettier, more talented or more worthy although I confess, it's a temptation to think so.

Many actors who read this book are just starting and will be scanning the list for agents who seem to be building their lists or who work free-lance extensively. There are many of those agents who have great potential. There are some who don't.

You might only be able to attract a one man/woman office, yet if that agent is the *right* person, he/she could make you a star whereas the most prestigious conglomerate might leave you dying on the vine. The most important office in town might sign you even without your union card, if your look excites them. That's rare, but it does happen.

Like attracts like. You will ultimately get just what you want in an agent. I believe you can get a terrific agent. I believe you can be a terrific client.

Write this on your wall someplace:

There are no shortcuts.

Today is not the last day of my life.

Agency Listings

Words to remember:

1. Your first agent is yourself. You must agent yourself until you attract someone who will care, and who has more access than you. It's better to keep on being your own agent than to have an agent who either does not know anything or doesn't care.

2. Mass mailings are usually a waste of money. There is no use sending your picture blindly to someone you never heard of. Although most agencies *do* glance at pictures and resumes, they get a lot of laughs out of them, too. If there is no consciousness regarding the appropriateness of the submission, it's clear to them that you do not know what you are doing. If you have no access to information about the agent, how do you know you want him? Be selective.

3. Read all the listings before you make a decision. If you find agents who interest you, look in the index and see if they are quoted. If so, this will give you even more information. Cull your list to five, if none of those five are interested, you can go back and choose some more.

4. Getting the right agent is not the answer to all your prayers—but, it is a start! Good luck

About Talent Inc.

37 East 28th Street, #408
btwn Madison & Park Avenues
New York, NY 10016
212-889-8284

Lally, Rogers & Lerman, Inc. is no more. Amicably
deciding to go their own way, Wallace Rogers and Peter
Lerman retained the space and Dale moved to Ninth
Avenue to open LTA/Lally Talent Agency.

Although they do book actors on occasion, About Talent,
Inc. reflects Wallace and Peter's successful origins in the
print agency business.

Agents
Wallace Rogers and Peter Lerman.
Client List
free-lance
Clients
free-lance
Notes

Abrams Artists & Associates, Ltd.

420 Madison Ave, S 14th Floor
at 47th Street
New York, NY 10017
212-935-8980

A brusk, efficient man, Harry Abrams has headed or partnered a string of agencies over the years; Abrams-Rubaloff, one of *the* commercial forces in New York City in the late 1960's and 1970s, Abrams/Harris & Goldberg, a prestigious theatrical agency in Los Angeles during the early to mid 1980s and currently Abrams Artists both in New York and Los Angeles. Through resourcefulness, determination and the hiring of excellent theatrical agents with their own splendid client lists, Harry has carved out an impressive New York agency that is well-thought-of both in all areas of the business.

The respected children's agency, Kronick, Kelly and Lauren joined Abrams in 1990 giving Abrams Artists & Associates, Ltd., even more credibility. Mr. Abrams is headquartered on the west coast, but is very much in touch with everyday business.

Because Abrams was reluctant to provide information about the agency, I am not publishing client names, but it is an easy thing for you to check out with SAG lists.

Agents
Neal Altman, Tracy Goldblum, David Evans, Robert Attermann, Meg Bloom, Cesca Cecelio, Ruthanne Secunda, Robert Kolker, Lexy Spett, Christina DeVries, Ellen Gilbert, Robert McCarthy and Fran B. Miller.

Client List
Check SAG listings or <u>The Players Guide.</u>
Clients
Same song
Notes

Drop Resume by in person.

Sent 2/23   Robert Kolker

The Actor's Group Agency

157 W 57th Street, Suite 604
btwn 6th & 7th Avenues
New York, NY 10019
212-245-2930

Pat House's 1968 decision to give up acting and join
Stewart Artists representing such models-becoming-actors as
Cybil Shepherd and Susan Dey was just the beginning of a
career spent nurturing actors. Pat worked with Wilhelmina
and Harry Abrams before joining Michael Slessinger at The
Actors Group in 1982.

When Michael moved to Los Angeles in 1984, he left the
New York office in Pat's hands. She now owns The
Actor's Group and Michael's company (now only in Los
Angeles) is called The Michael Slessinger Agency. The
agency has continued to grow in access and stature and with
the addition of colleague, Charles Kopelman, The Actors
Group now represents directors as well. AG looks at
pictures and free-lances on a very limited basis.

Agents
Pat House and Charles Kopelman.
Client List
65
Clients
Jana Schneider, Michael Cumpsty, Janet Hubert and others.
Notes

Bret Adams

448 W 44th Street
btwn 9th & 10th Avenues
New York, NY 10036
212-765-5630

If it's a job in the theater, Bret Adams has probably done it.
From acting (films & off-Broadway) to producing (theater
in Australia) to publicity and stage managing (for Equity)
Bret has cut a varied path to his life today as one of the
most reputable independent agents in New York. In the
early days, he worked with Sanford Leigh, Dick Voidts and
Marje Fields before opening his own agency in 1971.
Bret's partner since 1982, Mary Hardin's credentials were
forged living the gypsy life of a regional theater director's
wife. Since that life required moving every six months,
Mary acquired a resume (and contacts) at theaters across the
land doing whatever job was available. Bret Adams and
Mary Hardin are two of the most respected agents in the
business. Margi Rountree and Nancy Curtis are colleagues.

Agents
Bret Adams, Mary Hardin, Nancy Curtis and Margi
Rountree.
Client List
100
Clients
Judy Kaye, Ron Holgate and others.
Notes

AFA

Agents for the Arts
203 W 23rd Street
btwn 7th & 8th Avenues
New York, NY 10011
212-229-2562

Quadruple threat actress-singer-production stage manager-director Carole Russo, arrived in New York ready for work as a performer, but quickly realized she didn't have the emotional stamina for it. She chose the next best thing and uses her background to represent and nurture her list of clients. Carole represented models at Paul Wagner Agency and others before realizing she preferred to put her theatrical background to what she terms *a more creative challenge*.

When she switched to the theatrical arena, her mentor was Fifi Oscard for whom she worked for five years. She has about 45 signed clients, but works with free-lance actors as well. Associate Scott McNulty deals mostly with commercials, industrials and young people.

Agents
Carole Russo and Scott McNulty.
Client List
45
Clients
Jack Daddoub, Wanda Richert, Kirby Ward, Beverly Ward and J. C. Alten.
Notes

Alliance Agency

1501 Broadway, #404
btwn 43rd & 44th Streets
New York, NY 10036
212-840-6868

Alliance Agency is the new mid-size agency that resulted
from the merger of some of New York's brightest and most
effective agents. Craig Dorfman of The New York
Agency, Allen Flannagan of The Allen Flannagan Agency
(originally partnered with Michael Kingman) and Molly
McCarthy (Writers & Artists and Select Artists
Representatives, Inc.) have collaborated to form the newest
New York answer to the growing mega-agencies.

Craig was a company manager and a general manager
before he became an agent with The Leaverton Agency and
Allen was always considered a *balancing personality with a
great eye for talent* when he was in business with Michael
Kingman. Molly McCarthy was a child actor who grew up
to become a respected acting teacher and coach. She not
only has impeccable credentials, but is one of the most
gracious and charming agents I've interviewed. Joy
Trapani and Jim Flynn were Craig's assistants at the New
York Agency and are now subagents at The Alliance
Agency.

These agents have long enjoyed warm relationships with the
casting community. Their combined contacts can only
enhance clients' entre.

Agents
Craig Dorfman, Allen Flannagan, Molly McCarthy, Joy Trapani and Jim Flynn.

Client List
100

Clients
Doris Belack, Tom Calabro, Joan Copeland, Wendy Makkena, S. Epatha Merkerson, Park Overall and others.

Notes

Sent 2/23 Jim Flynn

Ambrosio/Mortimer

165 W 46th Street, # 1109
E of Broadway
New York, NY 10038
212-719-1677

Louis Ambrosio's background gives him perspective for life
as an agent since he has been on both sides of the table. A
man with a Masters in Twentieth Century Literature and an
MFA in directing and management, he started his own
theater in 1973 and ran it successfully until 1980 at which
time he wrote the National Arts Endowment Policy.

In 1981, he started his own theatrical agency in New York
using his clients from regional theater days as a talent base.
In 1984 Meg Mortimer left William Morris to become
Louis' partner. Louis now heads the Los Angeles office
while Meg and colleague, Sarah Fargo operate the New
York office. A widely respected and very effective agency.

Agents
Meg Mortimer and Sarah Fargo.
Client List
200 - both coasts
Clients
Check SAG listings or The Players Guide.
Notes

Beverly Anderson

1501 Broadway, # 2008
btwn 43rd & 44th Streets
New York, NY 10036
212-944-7773

In a time when theater is dead and musical theater
nonexistent, Beverly Anderson still manages to earn the
bulk of her money by being one of the key agents in this
area. A colorful, candid lady who was an actress herself
until she tired of life on the road, Beverly has the
distinction of having turned down Barbara Streisand twice.
Her career began in 1956 at Dale Garrick Modeling. At
Garrick, which was a models-only agency, Beverly
suggested checking out some of the beauties to see if they
could talk a bit and qualify for The Jackie Gleason and
Steve Allen shows. She ended up booking consistently and
joined Jan Welsh (an Equity agent), where her first
submission placed Earl Sindor into a classic of the
American Theater, "Sweet Bird of Youth". Beverly has
had her own agency for over 20 years. She currently has
two agents in training: Rob Attea and Vicky Martin. Her
list of signed clients is short, but she works extensively with
free-lance talent. Beverly has fascinating quotes elsewhere
in the book.

Agents
Beverly Anderson.
Client List
20
Clients
Leonard Jackson, Vivica Lindfors and Al Lewis.
Notes

Andreadis Talent Agency, Inc.

119 West 57th Street, # 813
E of 7th Avenue
New York, NY 10019
212-315-0303

Like many actresses, Barbara Andreadis left the business when she had children. The kids are grown now and instead of continuing as an actress, Barbara is continuing as a mother, but this time, she has a larger family — of *actors* who, of course will *always* need her. When she decided to return to the business as an agent, Barbara trained at Bonnie Kidd. She ended up running the agency for two years before starting her own business in 1983.

Barbara says she *carries no generic type, only individuals* and has clients on soaps as well as on Broadway and in film and television. Representative clients include Kelly Ripa ("All My Children"), Ryan Phillipe ("One Life to Live"), Pamela Everett ("The Hudsucker Proxy") Penny Ayn Maas ("Crazy for You"), Melissa Haizlip ("Jelly's Last Jam"), Greg Ramos ("West Side Story") and Robert Jensen ("Secret Garden").

Sallee Held (who had an agency with Richard Dickens) has joined Barbara in representing a list of actors, singers and dancers. Although Barbara looks at all pictures and resumes, she usually sees people only by referral. LA liaison is The Light Company.

Agents
Barbara Andreadis.
Client List
35 + very little free-lance
Clients
Kelly Ripa, Ryan Phillipe, Pamela Everett, Penny Ayn Maas, Melissa Haizlip, Greg Ramos, Robert Jensen and others.
Notes

APA

Agency for the Performing Arts
888 Seventh Avenue
btwn 56th & 56th Streets
New York, NY 10106
212-582-1500

APA has taken a lot of hits lately. In Los Angeles, powerful John Gaines and beloved president, Marty Klein died in 1992 and Tom Korman and Larry Masser joined The Artists Group. The agency, at this point, is describing itself as a *mid-level* agency and is struggling to focus. Since APA was originally formed as an agency to represent artists for personal appearances, this area will continue to be its strong point. The New York office has new personnel as well. One of the agencies reaping rewards from the Triad/William Morris merger, APA signed up a few orphans who either did not make the cut or who preferred a folksier touch than that available with a large conglomerate. The list of agents servicing clients at APA is classy as well. Katy Rothaker came over after a 14 year stint at William Morris to head up the legit department. David Kalodner (The Kaplan Agency) remains at APA and is joined by Ed Betz from The Lantz Office.

Agents
Katy Rothaker, David Kalodner and Edward Betz.
Client List
Large
Clients
Tony Roberts, Bernadette Peters, Tony Lo Bianco, Rex Smith, Diane Venora, Jack Warden, Nancy Marchand, David Shiner, Robert Clohessy, Madeline Kahn and others.
Notes

Artists Group East

1650 Broadway, #711
at 51st Street
New York, NY 10019
212-586-1452

If you are lucky enough to end up with Robert Malcolm for an agent, my feeling is that you have not only found a tenacious, professional, patient, honest, tasteful, and caring agent but, a lifelong friend as well. Robert came to agenting in a fairly circuitous way. Originally an actor, Robert was coerced by his former agent into coming into business with her (The Peggy Grant Agency). She promised time off for auditions, but when Peggy died a few months later, she left the agency to Robert and he has not been to an audition since. Instead, not only has the agency grown in size and stature, but Robert has merged with The Artists Group in Los Angeles and now makes his home in that city. There are nine theatrical agents in the Los Angeles office and the agency is booming. Clients from Artists Group East in New York will find their entre enhanced by the new partnership with the thriving LA agency. Laz Pujol runs the New York office and makes sure that although Robert is no longer in New York that clients are well taken care of.

Agents
Robert Malcolm.
Client List
100
Clients
Pamela Payton-Wright, Patricia Connolly and others.
Notes

Richard Astor

1697 Broadway, # 504
btwn 53rd & 54th Streets
New York, NY 10019
212-581-1970

An old-line class-act, Richard Astor is one of my favorites.
I remember how nice he was to me when I came in off the
street as a beginning actor to drop a picture and resume.
The man has class, stature, access, and taste and a keen eye
for talent; Martin Sheen, Gene Hackman, Robert Duvall
and Nell Carter are only a few of the actors represented by
Richard early in their careers. Richard began his career as
an actor in 1957, but a work-related back injury forced him
to leave acting, so New York State's Workmen's Compensation trained him for a new career. Because Richard knew
he wanted to be an agent, he chose typing and speedwriting.
He assisted agent, Henry C. Brown and then worked for
Lily Veidt and Harriet Kaplan before opening his own
agency in 1960. Robert Frye (Spotlight and J. Michael
Bloom) joins Richard in nourishing and tracking talented
actors. Save your pictures and postage, Richard and Robert
find new clients by constantly tracking showcases and
theater. If you do the work, they will find you.

Agents
Richard Astor and Robert Frye.
Client List
30
Clients
Danny Aiello, David Patrick Kelly, Vivian Reed,
Rutanya Alda, Luis Guzman and others.
Notes

Drop by

174

Bauman, Hiller & Associates

250 W 57th Street
at Broadway
New York, NY 10019
212-757-0098

The style of this respected old-line agency on both coasts is comfortable and easy. Serious about business and light-hearted about life, west coast partners Dick Bauman and Wally Hiller have chosen affable Mark Redanty to head the New York office. Mark got his first taste of the business when he interned at Ragland-Shamsky while he was in college. After he completed his education, he pursued things before the lure of show business called him back to work with Richard Astor.

He has been the head of the New York office of Bauman Hiller & Associates since 1987 and is joined by colleague Victor Latino (PGA) in representing an important and respected list of clients. Bauman Hiller & Associates work free-lance only as a prelude to signing.

Agents
Mark Redanty and Victor Latino.
Client List
80
Clients
Robert Morse, Sada Thompson, Scott Wise, Peter Frechette and others.
Notes

Barry Haft Brown Artists Agency

165 W 46th Street, #2223
btwn 6th & 7th Avenues
New York, NY 10019
212-869-9310

One of the most productive and on-the-build agencies in
town is Barry Haft Brown. Bob Barry has had his own
agency for 33 years (The Barry Agency). In late 1991,
Bob, whose discerning eye uncovered former clients Gene
Hackman and Harvey Kietel, joined with former colleague
Nanci Brown (The Gersh Agency) and Steven Haft
(Ambrosio Mortimer) to produce a hot new force on the
New York agency scene. Nanci opened the Los Angeles
office in December of 1992 and reps the 40-50 clients who
work in LA while Haft and Barry rep the 75-80 clients in
New York.

Steven Haft's first job in the business was at Cunningham,
Escott, Dipene & Associates. When he decided to be an
agent, he joined Ambrosio Mortimer where he became
franchised. He worked with A-M in New York and Los
Angeles, so he understands how the business works on both
coasts. BHB's clients work in the theater, films, soaps, and
in all areas of television.

This agency only works with signed clients.

Agents
Bob Barry, Nanci Brown, Steven Haft.
Client List
75-80
Clients
John Spencer, Louis Arlt, Jordon Rhodes, Kim Cea, Dana Vance, Katherine Wallach, Ann Hamilton and others.
Notes

J. Michael Bloom

233 Park Avenue S
at 19th Street
New York, NY 10003
212-529-5800/212-529-6500

Former actor J. Michael Bloom was an agent with Sanford
Leigh when I came to New York. He has since parlayed
himself into one of the most important commercial agents in
town and built an impressive theatrical client list as well.
Michael is headquarted in Los Angeles tending to film
clients, but the New York team (headed by Brian Riordan)
definitely has things under control.

Brian Riordan's agenting career has only been at the top-of-
the-line. His first job was as a literary agent with
prestigious Phyllis Wender (now Rosenstone/Wender). His
career representing actors began at STE (now Paradigm)
and he has headed the theatrical department at J. Michael
Bloom since 1986.

Brian is joined by Elin Flack (Abrams Artists, Lionel
Larner) and Mark Schlegel (Ambrosio Mortimer)
representing such visible actors as William Baldwin, Sir
Alec Guinness, Anthony LaPaglia, Marsha Gay Hardin,
Joanna Going and Jonathan Price. Peter Levine (Marvin
Starkman, Susan Smith) has joined the Los Angeles office.
There is an impressive *youth* legit department at this agency
run by Rob Claus and Mark Upchurch.

J. Michael Bloom & Associates is an important liaison to
the British marketplace not only representing British stars in
America, but providing a connection between American

clients and British representation.

The physical splendor of this office is almost irresistible. I can imagine an actor dutifully interviewing agents and reviewing data in order to make an intelligent decision; getting off the elevator, taking one look at the sumptuousness of the office and at Michael's name in 12-foot-tall letters (only a slight exaggeration) holding out his pictures and saying, *Sign me.* Luckily this office has credibility, a great list and terrific agents.

Both the adult and youth legit departments haunt showcases, schools and the local theatrical scene on the lookout for talent in all age ranges.

Agents
Elin Flack, Brian Riordan, Mark Schlegel, Rob Claus and Mark Upchurch.
Client List
150
Clients
William Baldwin, Anthony LaPaglia, Marsha Gay Hardin, Joanna Going, Jonathan Price, Nigel Hawthorne, Sir Alec Guinness, Barnard Hughes, Anthony Heald, Boyd Gaines, Bob Westenberg, Laura Linney and others.
Notes

Sent 2/23   ~~MICHAEL~~ BRIAN RIORDAN (Legit Adults)
MICHAEL SHERA (Commercials)

Peter Beilin Agency, Inc.

230 Park Avenue, #1223
Pan Am Building
New York, NY 10169
212-949-9119

Peter Beilin was my commercial agent years ago at Abrams
Rubaloff. A talented and determined man, I was not
surprised that he started his own agency when A-R split in
1977. What *did* surprise me is that Peter's old rolodex is
still in tact. He still had my old New York phone number!

A musician who was afraid choosing music as his livelihood
would diminish its joy for him, Peter was a page at ABC
and quickly became the Night Program Manager: *The guy
they leave in charge when the important people go home.*
He produced for a while before crossing paths with Noel
Rubaloff who inspired him to become an agent.

Eighty-five percent of the work at this agency is
commercials, but they also do work for television. PBA
has celebrity clients for commercials (Richard Kiley, Ann
Reinking, Hulk Hogan and others) and also works
extensively with free-lance talent. Suzy Freidman is Peter's
associate.

Agents
Peter Beilin and Suzanne Freidman.
Client List
free-lance
Clients
Richard Kiley, Ann Reinking, Hulk Hogan and others.
Notes

Bookers, Inc.

150 5th Avenue #834
at 20th Street
New York, NY 10011
212-645-9706

Tim Ousey (pronounce Oh-Z) and his mother Joan are
Bookers, Inc. Although Tim looks to be 21 or so, he
swears to me that he's had time so far for an acting career
and five and a half years as an agent at Funny Face before
opening Bookers in 1986. Bookers handles kids, adults,
print, television, film, but no theater or voice overs.
Working from a pool of 300, Tim has a signed list of about
20. He tells me his clients do all the New York magazine
covers. Tim looks at all pictures and is happy to get
postcards from actors.

Agents
Tim Ousey and Joan Ousey.
Client List
20 + free-lance
Clients
Check SAG listings or The Players Guide.
Notes

Don Buchwald & Associates

10 E 44th Street
just E of 5th Avenue
New York, NY 10017
212-867-1000/1070

Ex-actor/producer Don Buchwald got his first job agenting
with Monty Silver in 1964. He joined the prestigious
commercial agency, Abrams-Rubaloff before starting his
own agency when A-R split. A brilliant negotiator and a
shrewd agent, Buchwald has built an impressive list of
clients *and* agents. Buchwald now has a Los Angeles
office.

Agents
Don Buchwald, David Williams, Ricki Olshan, Joanne Nici,
Richard Basch, Renee Jennett, Kristin Miller and William
Rue.
Client List
300 +
Clients
Check SAG listings or The Players Guide.
Notes

Carry Company Talent Representatives

1501 Broadway, #1408
btwn 43rd & 44th Streets
New York, NY 10036
212-768-2793

Sharon Carry and Robert Kunsmen are the heart and soul of
The Carry Company. More than just owners and partners,
Sharon and Robert are committed to making the business
part of acting a little less painful. Sharon, an actress, from
a showbiz family, had experienced and witnessed
actor/agent and actor/casting director relationships over a
long period of time and felt *there must be a better way* of
interaction. Unable to change things as an actor, this was
her first priority as an agent. Robert was a disc jockey in
Bethlehem, PA and Asbury Park, NJ before joining Sharon
in the plight to represent actors without pain. From the
interaction I observed when I was in their office, Robert
and Sharon's approach is more than just talk. The Carry
Company was established in early 1991.

Sharon's agent training is from the modeling/print side of
the business. An agency that the casting community takes
seriously, CC has a few signed clients, but works primarily
on a free-lance basis before taking on responsibility for a
career.

The Carry Company has a pool of about 120 kids and 50
adults. Don't *postcard* this agency unless you have
something real to say, *Hello, how are you* doesn't count.
They prefer flyers when you are doing something. The
Carry Company takes flyers and work very seriously.

Agents
Sharon Carry and Robert Kunsman.
Client List
170
Clients
free-lance
Notes

Carson-Adler Agency, Inc.

250 W 57th Street
at Broadway
New York, NY 10107
212-307-1882

One of the most respected children's agencies in New York
is run by Nancy Carson and Marion Adler. Nancy came to
the business through her daughter who is an actress. Being
a *stage mother* showed her a side of the business most
agents never experience. She worked as an agent for years
representing children at Jan J. Agency, before joining with
Marion to form C-A. Marion worked previously at MMG.
Today, Marion runs the successful commercial division
while Nancy is the place to shop for talented trained young
legit actors. A few from her list include Kelsey Scott, Alex
Ruiz, Johnny Pinto, Rachel Bella and David Krumholtz.
When she started naming her clients, it occurred to me that
every film, television and legit casting director must have
C-A as a key resource for young talent. The agency has 75
signed clients for theater, film, and television. Carson-
Adler looks at all pictures. They need not be professionally
done to be considered.

Nancy has written the definitive "How To" book for young
actors and their moms seeking work in the business. <u>Kid
Biz</u> is available at most bookstores. The book answers any
questions about this area of the business. I highly
recommend it.

Agents
Nancy Carson, Marion Adler Cynthia Katz and Karen
Apicella.
Client List
60
Clients
Matthew Branton, Kelsey Scott, Alex Ruiz, Johnny Pinto,
Rachel Bella, David Krumholt, Jessica DiCicco and others.
Notes

The Carson Organization

Helen Hayes Theater Bldg.
240 W 44th Street PH
btwn Broadway & 8th Avenue
New York, NY 10036
212-221-1517

Steve Carson and wife, Maria Burton-Carson opened The Carson Organization in late 1992 and from the looks of things, they're going to be around for a long time. As the daughter of Elizabeth Taylor and Richard Burton, Maria brings a certain overview to the business and Steve's background at New York agencies (Gilchrist, Phoenix, etc.) combine to make this agency a good choice for actors under age 30 who are looking for a home. Although Steve, Maria and colleague Victoria Kress (Triad) do represent the occasional free-lance client, their committment is to their signed clients who are all doing well in film, theater and television evidenced by Ian Ziering ("Beverly Hills 90210"), Shawn Thompson ("The Heights"), Jesse Cameron ("Slaughter of the Innocents") and Gabe Carmouch who is a regular on "Big Brother Jake". Steve says they look at all pictures and resumes and have found some of the most important people on his list from the mail.

Agents
Steve Carson, Maria Burton-Carson and Victoria Kress.
Client List
30 + very little free-lance
Clients
Ian Ziering, Shawn Thompson, Jesse Cameron, Gabe Carmouch and others.
Notes

MAIL Resumé - don't drop by
2/93 STEVE CARSON

Coleman-Rosenberg

210 E 58th Street
btwn 2nd & 3rd Avenues
New York, NY 10019
212-838-0734

Deborah Coleman and Jack Rosenberg started this agency in the 50s to represent actors, choreographers, writers and directors. This small anonymous agency purposefully manages to remain so though their clients are distinguished and visible.

Because the list is intentionally small, clients receive close attention and nurturing. Helping Coleman and Rosenberg nurture is associate, Ellison K. Goldberg. When former boss, Bonni Allen closed her agency and moved west, Ellison moved east (from Broadway to 58th Street) and everyone seems to be happy with the move.

Names from their list include Jean Stapleton and Gerald Freedman. C-R looks at all pictures and resumes but prefers (as do most agents) to choose their clients by seeing them work.

Agents
Deborah Coleman and Ellison K. Goldberg.
Client List
35-40
Clients
Jean Stapleton, Austin Pendelton, Donald Sadler, Gerald Freedman and others.
Notes

Douglas, Gorman, Rothacker & Wilhelm, Inc. (DGRW)

1501 Broadway, #703
btwn 43rd & 44th Streets
New York, NY 10036
212-382-2000

Douglas, Gorman, Rothacker and Wilhelm, Inc. was
established in 1988 when Fred Gorman (Bret Adams) joined
Flo Rothacker (Ann Wright), Jim Wilhelm (Lionel Larner,
Eric Ross, The Barry Douglas Agency) and Barry Douglas
(ICM) to form a New York mini-conglomerate that is
congenial *and* well connected.

Although this agency has grown in stature and access, it has
not sacrificed the nurturing elements that made it special to
actors in the first place, Flo Rothacker still has the
sensibilities that made her choose her first job at Ann
Wright's agency because of it's proximity to Bloomingdales
and she endures as one of New York's major musical
comedy agents. Former writer Barry's stints with ICM on
both coasts continually give him an edge in negotiating
tough contracts for clients and he has now joined forces
with Fred to guide a growing literary department. Jim's
eclectic background continues to inform his relationships
with clients.

Flo and Barry are quoted at length throughout the book. I
didn't spend time with either Fred or Jim, but their lineage
and current association makes them good choices as well.
DGRW also represents directors, choreographers, and
musical directors. Their Los Angeles liaison is Badgeley
and Connor. This agency looks at all mail and is
conscientious about covering showcases. They will look at

audition tapes if they are clips of professional work (not material that you have recorded on your own). Robyne Kintz is their colleague.

Agents
Barry Douglas, Fred Gorman, Flo Rothacker, Jim Wilhelm, and Robyne Kintz.
Client List
120
Clients
Ned Eisenberg, Dan Lauria, Roddy McDowell, Olivia De Havilland, Giancarlo Esposito, John Schuck, Phyllis Newman, Laurie Beechman and others.
Notes

David Drummond Talent Representation

102 W 75th Street
W of Columbus Avenue
New York, NY 10023
212-877-6753

David Drummond was an English actor who fell in love
with New York when he was on tour here and decided to
stay. He began working as a talent agent at William Morris
Agency and Dulcina Eisen before opening his own office in
the mid 80s. The office is international with Australian,
Jennifer Barbour (SCM&M, Triad, William Morris) joining
Drummond in 1992. Bernard Leibhaber previously worked
with Jerry Kahn. Drummond, Liebhaber and Barbour
represent actors, but do have a musical director and a
dramaturge on their list. Confidential about their list,
you'll have to check the SAG listings to see who their
clients are. Virginia Wilhelm assists the agents here and
John McKellar is their office manager.

Agents
David Drummond, Bernard Liebhaber and Jennifer
Barbour.
Client List
65
Clients
Check SAG listings or The Players Guide.
Notes

Eisenberg Aqua Hart

145 Avenue of the Americas
below Houston
New York, NY 10013
212-929-8472

David Eisenberg came to New York from California and worked in personnel before starting his agent career with Bob Waters. He also worked for Jan J. before moving to run the theater, film and television department for children and young adults at SCM&M. Ellen Aqua Hart was a casting assistant before joining SCM&M and soon became David's partner there. When SCM&M decided they only wanted to handle commercials, David and Ellen had their own business and only needed to find space, so in August 1991, when other agencies were biting the dust, Eisenberg Aqua Hart opened and has prospered. This agency specializes in kids and teens to age 20 for theater, film and television as well as commercials. Some clients include Jason Biggs ("Conversations with My Father", "Drexel's Class") and Alex Germain ("Chicken Soup"). Although this office works with babies, they do not sign them.

Agents
David Eisenberg, Ellen Aqua Hart.
Client List
100
Clients
Jason Biggs, Deven Miller, Maggie Thom, Paul Treichler, Alex Germain and others.
Notes

Epstein-Wyckoff & Associates

311 W 43rd Street, #1401
btwn 8th & 9th Avenues
New York, NY 10001
212-586-9110

Gary Epstein merged with Sharon Ambrose to form
Phoenix/Ambrose. When Sharon left the business, Gary
merged with Los Angeles agent, Craig Wyckoff giving both
Epstein and Wyckoff visibility and representation for clients
on both coasts. Gary was still an actor when he began
answering phones for his agent, Mort Schwartz and
unexpectedly began what was to become a career as an
agent. He spent nine years with prestigious
Hesseltine/Baker Agency before opening his own agency
when Hesseltine retired and Baker died. Today Gary
represents not only actors, but writers and directors as well.
E-W sees clients mostly by referral, but checks pictures and
resumes. Randi Ross (DBA and J. Michael Bloom), Edie
Cuminale (Mort Schwartz, Lester Lewis, Actors Group)
and Mark Fleishman (whose background includes
performing, casting and managing) are Gary's colleagues.

Agents
Gary Epstein, Mark Fleishman, Randi Ross and Edie
Cuminale.
Client List
more than 10 less than a million
Clients
Check SAG listings or <u>The Players Guide</u>.
Notes

Marje Fields, Inc.

165 W 46th Street #909
E of Broadway
New York, NY 10036
212-764-5740

Marje Fields started her career when soap operas were still on the radio and she's still a force in the 90s. She became an agent with Chuck Tranum (TRH) representing actors for commercials. When she started her own agency, she represented actors only for commercials, but today her agency represents actors in all fields and has a thriving literary department as well.

Colleagues Dorothy Scott and Lee Buckler also represent actors. The agency looks at all pictures and resumes and will call in anyone they feel able to represent.

Agents
Marje Fields, Dorothy Scott and Lee Buckler.
Client List
free-lance + signed
Clients
free-lance
Notes

Sent 2/23 MARJE

Flick East-West Talents, Inc.

881 Seventh Avenue, #1110
at 57th Street
New York, NY 10019
212-307-1850

A boutique agency in the purest sense of the word, Flick East-West has a very small eclectic list of actors with a sprinkling of writer-directors. A spinoff of the modeling agency Click, both are owned by Francis Grill. Peg Donegan (J. Michael Bloom and Ford Models) floats between the Los Angeles and New York offices and is assisted in New York by Paige Hanson. Flick also has a commercial department run by Sean McKenna.

Agents
Peg Donegan.
Client List
50
Clients
Dianne Brill, Debbi Mazar, Karen Duffy and others.
Notes

Foster-Fell Talent

36 E 23rd Street, 8th Floor
E of 5th Avenue
New York, NY 10010
212-353-0300

At one time, this agency was the Frances Dill Agency and dealt exclusively with models for magazines and runway work. All that changed in 1969 when Frances died and Jeremy Foster-Fell made a 24 hour decision to buy the agency. Although the focus was primarily as before, Jeremy noticed that times were changing and determined to change with them. To that end, today, F-F has agreements with SAG, AFTRA and Equity, and represents actors across the board. Their signed client list is quite small, but their free-lance file is large and active. Most of the work in the agency is in the commercial field, but FF does find work for clients in other areas as well. Jeremy says he opens his own mail, so he sees everything that crosses his desk. The challenge, he asserts, is *to deal with it in an intelligent way*. Although there are two other agents here (Josh Samuels and Roger Jehenson), Jeremy is the only agent who deals with actors other than with commercials.

Agents
Jeremy Foster-Fell, Josh Samuels and Roger Jehenson.
Client List
free-lance
Clients
free-lance
Notes

Frontier Booking International, Inc.

1560 Broadway, #1110
at 46th Street
New York, NY 10019
212-221-0220

Frontier Booking is not only one of the largest rock agencies around (they handle Squeeze, Sting, R.E.M. and others), but they have a happening theatrical department as well. Ian Copeland started Frontier in 1979 for music clients and branched out into film, television and commercials in 1984. John Shea (SCM&M and Kronick, Kelly and Lauren) heads up the department that represents a hot list of young actors working in very prestigious venues: Mike Damus (the film version of "Lost in Yonkers"), Jonathan Kaplan (nominated for "Falsettos"), Joe Chrest ("King of the Hill"), Tracy Douglas (in the new Bill Cosby play). John's colleagues are Debra Madow (LW2 and William Schuller Agency) and Lisa Weinberg (whose previous career was in casting.) Frontier works with an extensive free-lance list as well as with signed clients.

Agents
John Shea, Debra Madow and Lisa Weinberg.
Client List
20 + free-lance
Clients
Mike Damus, Jonathan Kaplan, Joe Chrest, Tracy Douglas and others.
Notes

The Gage Group

315 W 57th Street, #4H
W of 8th Avenue
New York, NY 10019
212-541-5250

I know I'm biased, but these are my favorite agents. In fact, Phil Adelman, Steve Unger, Wendy Relkin, Martin Gage and Pete Kaiser *are* my agents. I live in California, but when I go to New York, these folk are there for me.

Phil Adelman is the ultimate hyphenate: elementary school teacher-director-musical director-composer-lyricist-quiz show writer. When you see Phil's quotes elsewhere in this book, you will get even more of a flavor about how the office operates, but for starters, he told me he would never think of releasing a client just because he wasn't getting work: *When a client of mine doesn't get work, I just figure the people who are doing the hiring are morons. I know when I take on a client that it's for life. I have so much faith in my own taste that I would never lose faith in a client.* Does this give you an idea of why The Gage Group is such a sought after agency?

Steven Unger worked with Debbie Brown Casting before joing the group and becoming Phil's respected associate. Wendy Relkin heads the commercial department and Pete Kaiser concentrates on industrials. A talented, cool group of people, there is such a warmth about them that I think the agency should be renamed The Gage *Family*.

Agents
Phil Adelman, Steve Unger, Wendy Relkin, Martin Gage
and Pete Kaiser.
Client List
65
Clients
Stephen Pearlman, Marcia Lewis, Jane Connell, Tammy
Grimes, K Callan, Walter Bobbie, Liz Callaway, John
Cunningham, Nancy Ringham and others.
Notes

The Gersh Agency New York

130 W 42nd Street, #2400
btwn 5th & 6th Avenues
New York, NY 10036
212-997-1818

The Gersh Agency New York was formed when David Guc (pronounce Gus), Scott Yoselow, Ellen Curren and Mary Meager decided to leave Don Buchwald & Associates to form a New York office for the prestigious Los Angeles firm Phil Gersh started long ago. The Gersh Agency New York has continued to add stature to the Gersh legend. David Guc, Ellen Curren, Robert Duva (The Lantz Office), Nicholas Evans, Jr. and Raelle Koota represent Gersh acting clients while partners, Scott (William Morris) represents writers and directors, Susan Morris is the book agent and Jennifer Lyne handles below the line clients. Mary Meager has since left to join The William Morris Agency. GANY prefers well-trained actors and is meticulous about monitoring new talent by attending showcases and readings. If you don't have a referral, concentrate on doing wonderful work in a showcase and ask them to come and see it.

Agents
Ellen Curren, David Guc, Susan Morris, Robert Duva, Raelle Koota, Nicholas Evans, Jr.
Client List
220 (NY/LA)
Clients
John Turturro, John Goodman, Leonard Nimoy, Patti Lupone and others.
Notes

The Gilchrist Talent Group

310 Madison Avenue
at 42nd Street
New York, NY 10173
212-692-9166

Pat Gilchrist used to be best known as the mom of *Mikey*,
the adorable kid from the Life cereal commercials. The
Gilchrists had seven other appealing Mikeys at home and
since they were all working in commercials, Pat decided to
start her own agency. She learned about agenting by
apprenticing at Rascal's Unlimited and with the
encouragement of her husband, Tom Gilchrist (an ex-cop)
started her own business in 1982. Now however, she is
known as the *Professional Mom/Agent* to some of film and
television's most visible teen and child stars. Gilchrist is
also an active booker of children/teens for commercials.
Carol Davis (Roseanne Kirk, Talent East) and Chip Laverly
(Talent East) are Pat's colleagues. GTG is constantly on
the lookout for new kids and religiously looks at all pictures
and resumes. No clients over age 25.

Agents
Pat Gilchrist, Carol Davis and Chip Laverly.
Client List
45-55
Clients
Check SAG listings or The Players Guide.
Notes

Peggy Hadley, Enterprises, Ltd.

250 W 57th Street
btwn 7th & 8th Avenues
New York, NY 10107
212-246-2166

An actor who left the business by choice, Peggy Hadley has never missed performing. When she was searching for a new career, fellow performer Fannie Flagg talked Peggy into becoming her manager. Peggy managed Fannie and four others until their careers drew them to the west coast. Peggy (a transplanted Kentuckian) felt she couldn't bear leaving the city to go with them, so she just added more actors to her list and became an agent. She has about 60-70 signed clients and works with many others free-lance. She handles only legit, no commercials. Her assistant is Lewis Trisi and Gloria B. O'Neill is her office manager.

When I asked Peggy for clients names, she said she didn't want to name any lest she leave someone out, so I chose a couple of names from her list.

Agents
Peggy Hadley.
Client List
60-70
Clients
Lou Myers, Dick Latessa and others.
Notes

Harter Manning Woo

36 E 22nd Street, 3rd Floor
btwn Park Avenue S
& Broadway
New York, NY 10010
212-529-4555

Harter Manning Woo acquired a partner and became
bicoastal in 1992. Patty Woo (Kass and Woo, The Woo
Agency, The Monty Silver Agency) joined the agency and
moved to California to run the west coast offices of Harter
Manning Woo. Ellen Manning was a dancer, *go-fer* and
casting assistant before assisting the late Bernard
Rubenstein, who she describes as *the kindest, nicest,
shrewdest man in the business.* A successful commercial
agent, Bernie not only trained Ellen for 9 months to be the
agent she is today, but left his business to her when he
died. The name was changed for legal reasons in 1983 to
The Manning Agency.

Barbara Harter became Ellen's partner in 1987 after stints
as a casting director for The Guiding Light and Jane Iredale
Associates. She agented for J. Michael Bloom heading up
the model portion of his business before opening Barbara
Harter & Associates in 1985. Combining Ellen's strength
with *real* people Barbara's background in the beauty side of
the business and Patty Woo's list and contacts with the legit
community has made the partners a triple threat.

The New York theatrical department is headed up by Diana
Doussant (APA) with help from colleagues Mary Collins (J.
Michael Bloom) and Andy Corren.

HMW has grown in strength theatrically and still maintains

its edge in the commercial and beauty areas of the business. Commercial agents are Paul Brown and Ellen Manning. The beauty side of the agency is represented by Karen McBain, Terry Wanamaker and Barbara Harter.

Agents
Ellen Manning, Barbara Harter, Mary Collins, Diana Doussant and Andy Corren.
Client List
100
Clients
Frank Ralter, Hal Robinson, John McGinnis, David Wasson, Herb Downer, Roger Bowen, Ebony Jo-Ann, Marcella Lowery, Ann Duquensney, Kirsti Carnahan and others.
Notes

Henderson/Hogan

850 Seventh Avenue #1003
btwn 56th & 57th Streets
New York, NY   10019
212-765-5190

Jerry Hogan runs the home office of Henderson/Hogan with taste and understanding. An actor who chose not to cope with the instability of the actor's life, Jerry worked as a private secretary to actress Margaret Leighton before his first job in the agency business at The Dudley, Field & Malone Agency. He was a commercial agent at United Talent before joining Maggie years ago. Maggie runs the Los Angeles office while Jerry shepherds his 60 plus signed New York clients. Although H/H prefers to work with signed clients, they do occasionally free-lance with former clients and/or old friends.

Agents
Jerry Hogan, Karen Kirsch, Andrew Greenman and Jean Walton.
Client List
60 +
Clients
Earl Hyman, Karen Valentine, Michael Learned and others.
Notes

Innovative Artists

1776 Broadway, #1810
at 45th Street
New York, NY 10019
212-315-4455

Ken Kaplan (Harry Abrams, Associated Artists, Ken Kaplan Agency, APA) opened this agency in 1991 as the New York edition of prestigious Los Angeles agency Harris and Goldberg. When H&G expanded adding prestigious Los Angeles literary agent, Frank Wuliger as a partner, Innovative Artists Talent and Literary Agency was chosen as a new name reflecting the changes.

(Howard) Goldberg left the business and Ken has now moved to Los Angeles to help (Scott) Harris, leaving Scott Landis as head of the agency in New York. The offices on both coasts are manned by the full complement of agents, revolving coastally, so that all clients benefit from the attention of each of the agents. Scott Harris, Ken Kaplan, Michelle Grant, Scott Landis (Susan Smith), Nevin Dolcefino (Gersh), David Rose (Harris and Goldberg) and Adinah Feldman (Harry Gold) are the travelling agents.

Innovative clients include Moira Kelly ("Chaplin", "The Cutting Edge") and Eddie Furlong ("Terminator 2").

Agents
Scott Landis, Ken Kaplan, Scott Harris, Nevin Dolcefino,
David Rose, Michelle Grant and Adinah Feldman.
Client List
150 +
Clients
Moira Kelly, Eddie Furlong, Lou Diamond Phillips, Estelle
Getty, Frank Langella, Carol Kane, Kadeem Hardison and
others.
Notes

ICM/International Creative Management

40 W 57th Street
W of 5th Avenue
New York, NY 10019
212-556-5600

Everyone far and wide knows that CAA (Creative Artists Agency) is absolutely the most powerful agency in the world. Or are they? In 1991, ICM made significant inroads when pivotal William Morris agents defected to ICM bringing significant clients (Julia Roberts, Tim Robbins, Angelica Huston) with them to join other big guns like Eddie Murphy and Arnold Schwarzenegger who were already in residence. Then, in the great agency shakeup of 1992, Bill Block, head of prestigious boutique, InterTalent, disbanded his agency and returned to ICM as head of the West Coast office.

Known to be less corporate than William Morris and CAA (that means everyone in the corporation does not have to be called in to review your latest contract), International Creative Management is described by insiders as a stylish, forward-thinking boutique operation. Headed by president Jim Wiatts, powerful ICM is intent on replacing powerful CAA as the number one talent agency in the world.

Number two in the current agent hierarchy, ICM is poised for combat and recently reclaimed Kim Bassinger.

Formed when Ashley-Famous and CMA merged in 1971, this agency has many, many clients and many, many agents. One of the most famous is powerful Sam Cohn who heads the New York office.

Agents
Lisa Loosemore, Boaty Boatwright, David Lewis,
Sam Cohn, Paul Martini, Andrea Eastman and Sue
Leibmann.

Client List
Very large

Clients
Julia Roberts, Kim Bassinger, Susan Sarandon, Michelle
Pfeiffer, Denzel Washington, Stephen Rea, Judy Davis,
Joan Plowright, Vanessa Redgrave, Ralph Bakshi, Rene
Balcer, Peter P. Benchley, Woody Allen, Garry Marshall,
Mike Nichols and many, many others.

Notes Anne Archer, J Bealls

Jerry Kahn, Inc.

853 7th Avenue
btwn 53rd & 54th Streets
New York, NY 10036
212-245-7317

In 1958 Jerry Kahn left his job as a press agent to join
Louis Maxwell Rosen and represent the likes of Dustin
Hoffman and Ron Leibman. He also worked with William
Schuller before opening his own office in 1968. Theater,
film, and television are the main thrusts of the agency
although Jerry has been known to book an occasional
commercial. An old-fashioned agent who is happy to rep a
small list and do it with care and integrity, Jerry didn't
know what I was talking about when I asked what his
biggest complaint about actors would be. Now, that's nice.

Agents
Jerry Kahn.
Client List
20-25
Clients
Will Hare, Karen Lynn Gorney and others.
Notes

Roseanne Kirk Agency

730 5th Avenue
at 57th Street
New York, NY 10019
212-317-3487

Roseanne Kirk and her late husband were personal
managers before Roseanne opened her own agency in 1979.
Her signed list of about 50 includes directors, writers,
choreographers and artistic directors.

Roseanne's enterprising clients, director Bob Kalfin and
actress Queen Esther have collaborated to produce a show
that Esther wrote for herself.

Roseanne's colleague, Michael DeLeo worked with Equity
and as a producer before joining the agency. Together they
oversee an eclectic collection of talent.

Agents
Roseanne Kirk and Michael DeLeo.
Client List
50
Clients
Sabion Glover, Teresa Burrell, Queen Esther Marrow,
Bob Kalfin and others.
Notes

The Krasny Office, Inc.

1501 Broadway, #1510
at 43rd Street
New York, NY 10019
212-730-8160

Gary Krasny has the perfect background to be an agent. He was an actor, a publicist for Berkeley Books, a story editor for Craig Anderson (after he left the Hudson Theater Guild) and worked for Theater Now (general managers for Broadway) where he was assistant to Norman Rothstein (who had been general manager for Craig). In 1985, he decided he was more empathetic with the artist than management and made the decision to become an agent. Gary honed his agency skills at various agencies around town until deciding to open his own agency in late 1991. He found office space not only in the same building, but on the same floor of the same building where he had worked with Craig Anderson many years before.

Gary started strongly (with 51 loyal clients) because the casting community rallied to his support. Norma Eisenbaum (Sharon Ambrose) and Mary Haggerty (Ann Wright) run the highly successful commercial, voice over and print department.

Colleague, Joseph Iacono's previous career was coaching executives at Princeton on motivation and goal setting. Once he made the decision to get into show business, he moved to California learning the business by working temp jobs at ICM and Fox. As a floater, he was available to any office who needed a worker. By now, he must know how *everything* works. He returned to New York and joined

The Krasny Office. In an unfavorable economic climate, this agency has managed not only to open and survive, but to thrive and grow.

The Krasny Office has liaison arrangements with several Los Angeles agents and managers.

Agents
Gary Krasny and Joe Iacono.
Client List
85
Clients
Carl Gordon, Addison Powell, Barry Newman, Lisa Pelican, Alan Feinstein and others.
Notes

Lucy Kroll Agency

2211 Broadway
at 79th Street
New York, NY 10024
212-877-0556

Located in the landmark Apthorp Apartments on Broadway
and 79th, the Lucy Kroll Agency lives up to its residence.
Distinguished and respected, Lucy was educated at Hunter
College, The School for Stage, and by teachers and
performers at the Moscow Art Theater under the aegis of
Stanislavski and Meyerhold. She also had classical ballet
training. In 1935, she was the co-founder of the American
Actors Company with Horton Foote, Agnes Demille and
others. In 1940 she became a story analyst at Warner
Brothers and co-founded the Hollywood Alliance. In 1945,
Sam Jaffe asked her to return to New York to open this
office, the forerunner to the Lucy Kroll Agency. For most
of the almost 50 years of the Lucy Kroll Agency, she has
run her agency as a one woman show, but times change and
so did Lucy. Realizing that she had an important legacy to
bestow (both for actors and for writers), Lucy began to
expand her agency in 1986. At that time, Barbara
Hogenson (who is now Lucy's partner) was leaving a
position as Director of Creative Research at Foote, Cone
and Belding. Barbara's background in research extended to
an interdisciplinary graduate degree in film, photography
and art library and a job at the Museum of Modern Art.
Lucy knew how valuable this type of person could be for
her agency.

Barbara oversees the office which has now grown to include
a total of five agents. Beth Gardiner joins Kroll after a

career with theatrical advertising agency, Russek Advertising. Holly Lebed has worked hard to build a stable of new young actors who complement long time clients like Uta Hagen, Kim Stanley, and James Earle Jones. They see prospective clients mainly from industry referrals.

Agents
Lucy Kroll, Barbara Hogenson, Holly Lebed, Zoe Lieberman and Beth Gardiner.
Client List
60
Clients
James Earl Jones, Ray Aranta, Brian Markinson, Paul Anthony Stewart, Uta Hagen, Kim Stanley and others.
Notes

Hilary EDSON

Kronick, Kelly & Lauren/Abrams Artists

420 Madison Avenue
btwn 48th & 49th Streets
New York, NY 10001
212-935-8980

Kronick, Kelly & Lauren, a successful children's talent
agency, recently merged with Abrams Associates, giving
Abrams a successful children's division and KKL an
important outlet for clients that age off their list.
Jane Kronick worked at a candy store before becoming an
agent with the Judy Kline Agency where she met fellow
agent, Jack Kelly. Ayn Lauren joined that agency (which
later became Kronick and Kelly) and left to work in the
children's department of J. Michael Bloom for a four years.
When Ayn returned in 1987 KKL was born. In July 1989
Jane sold her interest to Abrams and Jack became a casting
director. Robert McCarthy has inherited the crown and
now oversees the children. Although he specializes in
children, he says the print list *covers from birth to death*.
The list is quite large commercially and theatrically. They
look at all pictures and will look at snapshots of children.

Agents
Robert McCarthy, Fran B. Miller, Christina DeVries and
Ellen Gilbert.
Client List
200
Clients
Jessie Tendler, Avanti Taylor, Amir Williams
and others.
Notes

Lally Talent Agency (LTA)

Film Center Building
630 Ninth Avenue #800
at 44th Street
New York, NY 10036
212-974-8718

Dale Lally was an actor and a personal manager before he crossed the desk to became an agent. He worked for Mary Ellen White and Nobel Talent prior to becoming partners with print agents, Wallace Rogers and Peter Lerman (Lally Rogers & Lerman). Lally, Rogers and Wallace mutually decided to go their separate ways and Dale opened his own office in June of 1992.

Old friends from Noble Talent days, Heather Hawkins (she was a secretary there) and Dale reconnected just as he was putting LTA together and she is now his colleague. Although not related, Heather and Dale are *perfect twins*, born within moments of each other in 1948. Heather says this accounts for them being on the *same wave-length 23 hours a day*. Whatever the reason is, LTA is prospering in a down time. Dale and Heather think of LTA as a boutique agency, they have strong musical performers, interesting young adults and solid character people.

Agents
Dale Lally and Heather Hawkins.
Client List
20
Clients
Tom Flagg, Jim Lally (no relation), Teresa Wolf, Carol Harris, Judy Malloy, Brenda Denmark and others.
Notes

The Lantz Office

888 Seventh Ave.
btwn 56th & 57th Streets
New York, NY 10106
212-586-0200

The Lantz Office is one of the class acts in the annals of show biz. When I quizzed New York agents as to other agents they admired, Robert Lantz was the name most mentioned. He started in the business as a story editor. On a Los Angeles business trip from his London home in 1950, Phil Berg of the famous Berg-Allenbery Agency made him an offer he couldn't refuse, *Don't go home. Come to New York. Open a New York office for us.* Mr. Lantz did open the New York office at 3 East 57th Street and represented Clark Gable, Madeliene Carroll and other illustrious stars until William Morris bought that company a year later.

Lantz worked for smaller agencies for a few years before opening Robert Lantz, Ltd. in 1954. In 1955, he succumbed to Joe Mankiewicz's pleas and joined him producing film. It only took three years to figure out that he found agenting a much more interesting profession. In 1958, Lantz reentered the field as a literary agent. Feeling a mix of actors and directors and writers gave each segment more power, his list soon reflected that.

Dennis Aspland worked for the legendary Sam Cohn before joining Lantz in representing screenwriters and directors. Although this agency *does* major in writers and directors, they do represent actors, mostly long time clients.

Agents
Robert Lantz and Dennis Aspland.

Client List
20
Clients
Polly Holiday, B. D. Wong, Carol King, Elaine Stritch,
Elizabeth Taylor and a few others.
Notes

Lionel Larner, Ltd.

130 W 57th Street, 8G
btwn 6th & 7th Avenues
New York, NY 10019
212-246-3105

One of the classiest agents in town, both in demeanor and client list, Lionel Larner's first job in the business was as European casting director for Otto Preminger on the film St. Joan. When he turned in his casting hat for that of an agent, he was trained by powerful, Martin Baum (now one of the heads of CAA). In 1969 Lionel left Baum and GAC (now ICM) and started Lionel Larner, Ltd.

Not only did Lionel start at the top, he has remained there with prestigious clients like Glenda Jackson, Carroll O'Connor, and Stacy Keach. LL, Ltd. is not strictly a star agency, Lionel and colleague David Barison represent actors on every level.

Barison started out to be a dentist and got derailed interning at Gersh NY while still in school. He also pulled a few teeth at Abrams Artists before making his way to LL, Ltd. as an agent. David is low-key and wry, I really enjoyed talking to him even if he used to be a densist.

Lionel admits to being a real snob about his clients, demanding they have impeccable theater backgrounds. Well, why not? *He* does. One of the perks of this book has been meeting people like Lionel who return phone calls, are responsible, creative, caring and have taste, style, stature, and access.

Agents
Lionel Larner and David Barison.
Client List
40
Clients
Glenda Jackson, Carroll O'Connor, Dorothy Loudon, Stacy Keach, Madeleine Potter, Diana Rigg, Jack Weston and others.
Notes

Bruce Levy Agency

335 W 38th Street, #202
btwn 8th & 9th Avenues
New York, NY 10018
212-563-7079

Life is an adventure should be emblazoned on the forehead
of Bruce Levy. An actor, a producer ("The Price of
Genius") and an entrepreneur who can do anything, Bruce
Levy finally decided to put all those talents together and
open an agency. On *opening* day, October 2, 1992, Bruce
found himself up to his ears in work and in actors. A man
who doesn't know how to do things half way, Bruce gives
the kind of attention that has attracted actors with important
resumes. Motivated actors inspire him to even greater
heights. The office includes a well equipped theater in
which to view clients and would-be clients. Bruce is
interested in making money for himself and his clients, but
his motivation is quality. Actors with the same headset will
find a happy and rewarding relationship with the Bruce
Levy Agency.

Agents
Bruce Levy.
Client List
free-lance
Clients
free-lance
Notes

LW2 Talent Agency, Inc.

9 E 37th Street
btwn Madison & 5th Avenues
New York, NY 10016
212-787-2609

Although LW2 is primarily a commercial agency, they do submit the occasional picture for a soap if they feel one of their clients is right for it. LW1 in Los Angeles and LW2 in New York are the extensions of the old Wilhelmina Modeling Agency. Deiter and Gabby Esch had at one time been associated with The Light Agency and when they bought Wilhelmina, they joined initials of those two ventures for the two agencies. Though the agencies are completely separate, they do handle one anothers clients on a liaison basis. Carole Ingber, who runs the office was in advertising in 1982 when she decided to move to Los Angeles where she worked in casting with Vicki Rosenberg. When she came back to New York, she worked for J. Michael Bloom until SCM&M was formed with Bloom alumnae and she was invited to join them. She was hired by Dieter and Gabby to run LW3 in 1990 at the agency's debut. LW2 deals in commercials, voice overs and industrials.

Agents
Carole R. Ingber, Amy Lippman and David Chu.
Client List
150 + free-lance
Clients
Ann Pitoniak, Pam Clifford, Michelle Pawk, Armand Schultz and others.
Notes

William Morris Agency (Triad)

1350 Avenue of the Americas
at 54th Street
New York, NY 10019
212-586-5100

There really was a man named William Morris whostarted
this agency in 1898. The *IBM* of the conglomerate
agencies, WMA has recently gone through major
restructuring to compete with #1 (CAA) and #2 (ICM). In
its bid to transform, WMA merged in late 1992 with
prestigious Triad in order to capture more big name actors.
Jeff Hunter, Gene Parseghian (the NY partners of Triad),
Joanna Ross and Frank Frataroli join WMA agents, Johnny
Planco, Emily Gerson, Joan Fields, Bill Butler and Larry
Taube in representing their combined talent lists.

Their clients number well over a thousand. The office
employs 150 agents and 550 others in all branches, with
half of them working in the Beverly Hills office.
"William Morris Office at 85"
Ray Loynd
Variety
June 8, 1983

This dated article from Variety still pretty much tells the
WMA story and that number does include the many clients
the agency has other than actors (directors, producers,
writers, athletes, newscasters, political figures, Fawn Hall,
etc.) and the agents who rep this incredible variety. Their
agents probably have agents! If your career is heating up
and you are so inclined, the venerable WMA is now in the
position of *really* trying harder, since they are number

three. I'm told by my Los Angeles WMA friends that the word from on high is to *never take no for an answer* in pursuing a client's opportunities. The trick is to become the client WMA is looking to please. My knowledge of the Triad bunch leads me to believe chances of *person-to-person* treatment at WMA have greatly improved.

Mary Meager (Gersh/NY) recently joined this agency. More on the William Morris Agency in the chapter (9) on star agencies.

Agents
Jeff Hunter, Gene Parseghian, Johnny Planco, Frank Frataroli, Joanna Ross, Emily Gerson, Joan Fields, Bill Butler, Larry Taube and Mary Meager.
Client List
very large
Clients
Elizabeth Taylor, Clint Eastwood, Emma Thompson, Marisa Tomei, John Malkovich, Kevin Kline, Daniel Day Lewis, Morgan Freeman, Harvey Keitel, Matthew Modine, Mary Louise Parker and many, many others.
Notes

Nouvelle Talent, Inc.

20 Bethune Street, #3B
W of HB Studios/Bank St.
New York, NY 10014
212-645-0940

A Chicago agency with offices in New York and Las
Vegas, Ann Bordalo opened her New York office and
enlisted one of her clients to help her. B.G. Gross is talent
coodinator and runs seminars for the agency. Nouvelle
pursues employment in theater, film and television, as well
as corporate clients like Coca-Cola and Nabisco for
industrials and trade shows.

Proud of the fact that this is an agency run by women,
Nouvelle, nonetheless finds jobs for men as well. B.G.
says Ann looks at all the pictures that come in and that she
represents actors of all types and sizes from teenagers on
up. *The biggest thing keeping actors from working is not
following through,* says B.G. Her watch-words: *Make sure
the agent always has pictures and resumes at hand for a
quick submission, have a two minute monologue at-the-
ready, dress appropriately and have good honest
photographs.*

Agents
Ann Bordalo.
Client List
large
Clients
free-lance
Notes

Fifi Oscard Associates, Inc.

19 W 44th Street
just W of 5th Avenue
New York, NY 10036
212-764-1100

Fifi Oscard was a frustrated housewife and mother in 1949 when she began working gratis for Lee, Harris, Draper. When I asked her in what capacity she was working, she said, *mostly as a jerk* but added that in nine months she was no longer inept and had worked herself up to $15 a week. Always interested in theater and with the ability *to do almost anything*, Fifi has prospered. Fifi bought her own agency in 1959 and today holds forth over a giant agency that represents actors, directors, producers, singers, composers, writers - every arm of showbiz except the variety field. The agency handles about 120 signed clients for theater, film, and television and services free-lance people mainly in the courtship stage before signing them. Fifi continues to be the same warm, shrewd earth mother I encountered early in my career. Carmen LaVia heads the legit department, Barry Kolker shepherds juvenile clients. Fifi Oscard Associates looks at all pictures and resumes.

Agents
Eileen Haves, Carmen LeVia, John Medeiros, Francis Del Duca, Barry Kolker.
Client List
large
Clients
Ann Crum, Victoria Wyndam, Leon Redbone and others.
Notes

Harry Packwood Talent, Ltd.

250 W 57th Street, #2012
at Broadway
New York, NY 10107
212-586-8900

An actor on "The Patty Duke Show", Harry Packwood
made a life transition and became an agent. He opened the
agency with his mother, Doris Packwood and the two of
them run an efficient thriving office.

Doris and Harry see people mainly through referrals but do
look at all pictures and resumes. HPT is interested in
clients over the long haul and supports them by being
professional, energetic, caring, and personable.

The office works extensively with free-lance talent as well
as having a signed list of about 25.

Agents
Harry Packwood and Doris Packwood.
Client List
25 + free-lance
Clients
Barbara Passolt, Keith Perry and others.
Notes

Dorothy Palmer Talent Agency, Inc.

235 W 56th Street, #24K
btwn 7th & 8th Avenues
New York, NY, 10019
212-765-4280

Dorothy Palmer Talent Agency has 14,000 names in its
talent computer and 450 in its annual Palmer People Book.
Dorothy has about a dozen signed clients.

One would think with all these faces and resumes that the
proprietor here would be either out of her mind or totally
unapproachable. Neither is true. Dorothy, assisted by
Doris McCarthy, seems to not only have everything in hand
but to be pretty calm and together about things. She trained
with Sol Horok Enterprises and worked with National
Concert and Artists Corporation before starting her own
agency in 1974.

Agents
Dorothy Palmer.
Client List
12 + free-lance
Clients
J. J. Reap, Frank Gorshin, Captain Lou Albano and
others.
Notes

paradigm

200 W 57th Street, #900
btwn 7th Avenue & Broadway
New York, NY 10019
212-246-1030

This new human size conglomerate bills itself as, *paradigm, a talent and literary agency.* The amalgamation of four eminent New York and Los Angeles agencies, paradigm promises to be one of the more distinguished mergers benefiting not only the successful agents involved, but lucky clients as well. The wedding involves two elegant talent agencies (STE and Gores/Fields) and two heavy hitter literary agencies (Shorr Stille & Associates and Robinson/Weintraub & Gross). The original partners of New York's STE, Clifford Stevens, Tex Beha and David Eidenberg have reconfigured the agency. Clifford is now based in Los Angeles, Tex heads the New York office and David left the business to become a shrink.

A mainstay of the New York agency scene, this merger will add to the power, class and stature of this important agency. The New York theatrical agents include Tex Beha, concentrating on commercials and soaps and Richard Schmenner and Stephen Hirsh (Curtis Brown), long-time STE agents handle actors for theater, film and television. Claudia Black represents actors under 18. paradigm has clients in England as well as New York and Los Angeles. Mildred Dunnock has been Clifford's client since even before he had his own agency.

Agents
Tex Beha, Richard Schmenner, Stephen Hirsh and Claudia Black.
Client List
60
Clients
Mildred Dunnock, Jason Robards, Alfre Woodard, Penny Fuller and others.
Notes

Professional Artists Unlimited

513 W 54th Street, 2nd Floor
btwn 10th & 11th Avenues
New York, NY 10019
212-247-8770

Sheldon Lubliner is fun, he's easy to talk to, he's informed,
he is a good negotiator and has a good client list. Add
charm, taste, ability, access, and a great partner, Marilynn
Scott Murphy, and you've pretty much got a picture of
Professional Artists Unlimited. As a director-producer, he
enjoyed all the details involved in mounting shows for Al
Pacino, Gene Barry and Vivica Lindfors, he just didn't like
raising the money. At that point, he decided he could
transfer all his skills into agenting and not be a fundraiser.
His contacts and style translated into an agency called News
and Entertainment which he started in 1980. PAU is an
outgrowth of that venture. Actress/client, Marilynn Scott
Murphy was commandeered to answer phones in a pinch in
1983 and has since become Sheldon's partner. Sheldon's
negotiating skills combine with Marilynn's people skills,
although they are both strong in this department, *to form
the perfect agent*. Their client list includes not only actors,
newspersons, and radio personalities but also directors,
writers, producers and casting directors.

Agents
Sheldon Lubliner and Marilynn Scott Murphy.
Client List
100
Clients
Michael Constantine, Kim Coates, Betty Garrett and others.
Notes

Gilla Roos, Ltd.

16 W 22nd Street, 7th Floor
just W of 5th Avenue
New York, NY 10010
212-727-7820

Gilla Roos was an agent at Ann Wright before she started
her own commercial agency in 1974. Before that she had
worked at one of the first commercial/print agencies in
town (Sy Perkins). David Roos resisted his mother's pleas
to join the family business and became a chef until 1980
when finding himself between jobs, he finally succumbed.
David says he hasn't cooked since! Gilla died in 1989 and
David now heads the agency.

Marvin A. Josephson (APA) left the Hartig/Josephson
Agency in 1984 and opened the theater film and television
department of this office. Marvin deals with theater, film,
television, soaps, etc. Terri Bader (Gilchrist Agency)
handles kids and teens for theater, film and television as
well as commercials. A family affair, David's wife, Lynn
is the receptionist. Some of Roos' clients include Samuel
Wright (the voice of Sebastian the Crab) and Frank Vincent
("Jungle Fever" and "Honeymoon in Vegas". The office in
Los Angeles is run by Jeanette Walton.

Agents
David Roos, Marvin A. Josephson and Terri Bader.
Client List
100
Clients
Frank Vincent, Samuel Wright and others.
Notes

Shelly Rothman

101 W 57th Street, 11 E
at 6th Avenue
New York, NY 10019
212-246-2180

Shelly Rothman is one of the few variety agents still operating as an independent agent. Shelly became an agent by accident. Just out of the Navy in 1944, he landed a job as a *gofer* for a variety talent agency. Three years later he joined IFA as a variety agent booking comics and singers that work cabarets, nightclubs, the Catskills, etc.

Shelly works with a select list but has been known to help struggling performers by pointing them out to people who are interested in developing new talent.

Agents
Shelly Rothman.
Client List
28
Clients
Corbett Monica, Julius LaRosa, Rosemary Clooney, Sal Richards, Bob Melvin and others.
Notes

Sames & Rollnick Associates

250 W 57th Street, #703
at Broadway
New York, NY 10017
212-315-4434

Mary Sames and Diana Rollnick were colleagues at Gary
Leaverton when they decided to form Sames & Rollnick
Associates in 1985. Their client list continues to grow in
stature and credibility. When Bill Timms (The NY Agency
and Writers & Artists) joined S&R in 1991, he brought
over a raft of top musical performers so the list has grown.
Colleague, Linda Jacobs (Don Buchwald) joins Mary, Diana
and Bill. Sames and Rollnick and their cohorts are
successful, well-thought-of agents who appear to be
accessible, nurturing, and very connected to the lives of
their clients.

S&R free-lances only if they are interested in eventually
signing the client. Los Angeles agencies that have liaison
arrangements with S&R are The Artists Agency, Borinstein
Oreck Bogart and Gold/Marshak.

Agents
Mary Sames, Diana Rollnick, Linda Jacobs and Bill Timms.
Client List
80-95
Clients
Alma Cuervo, Rachel York, Henderson Forsyth, Maxwell
Caulfield, John McMartin, Jamey Sheridan, Stephen
Bogardus, Kelly Clark and others.
Notes
MAIL Resumé – don't drop by.

The Sanders Agency, Ltd.

1204 Broadway, #306
btwn 29th & 30th Streets
New York, NY 10001
212-779-3737

Honey Sanders was a working actress in 1978 when her
agent (Francie Hidden at Richard Pitman Agency) became
ill. Because Honey understood the business and liked
people, she volunteered to run the office. She'd already
been instrumental in landing jobs for lots of her friends, so
why not get paid for it? She divided her time between
agenting and acting when Francie recovered. When Francie
died, so did Honey's acting career as she made the full-time
switch to agenting.

Daughter Barbara runs the New York office, along with
Karen Garber (Joel Pitts) who heads up the commercial
department and Roger Lipson (William Shuller Agency)
who represents children and young adults. This agency
handles free-lance people as well as signed clients.

Agents
Barbara Sanders, Honey Sanders, Karen Garber and
Roger Lipson.
Client List
50
Clients
Check SAG listings or The Players Guide.
Notes

William Shill Agency, Inc.

250 W 57th Street, #2402
at Broadway
New York, NY 10019
212-315-5919

After working as a stage manager for 26 years, Bill Shill decided to take all the resourcefulness he had acquired and honed and use it to help actors get jobs instead of just making sure they got on stage at the right time!!

In 1984, Shill opened his own office and while continuing to work extensively with free-lance talent, Bill now has 20 signed theatrical and commercial clients. Bill's years of stage managing affect his *actor-perspective* and he feels it gives him an edge in spotting talent. He represents actors for theater, film and television.

Bill has interesting contributions elsewhere in the book regarding things actors can do to help themselves in the business.

Agents
William Shill.
Client List
20 + free-lance
Clients
Jeffrey Pomerantz, Larry Small, Scott Fowler, Cleo Kelly Conroy and others.
Notes

Select Artists Representatives

337 W 43rd Street, #1B
btwn 8th & 9th Avenues
New York, NY 10036
212-586-4300

Select Artists Representatives added personnel, clients and strength recently when they merged with Iannone-Day. Mary Day retired and Bill Iaonne and Kiel Junius joined Select creating a whole new *agent-family.*

Alan Willig, a former stage manager, became a protege of one of the greats in the agency business, Bob Baker (Hesseltine/Baker) in 1979. When Hesseltine retired and Baker died suddenly, Alan fell heir to the agency and changed the name to Alan Willig and Associates. Now known as Select Artists and with added partners, the agency continues to be a source of top line talent for casting directors and producers. Jacinthia Alexander is still part of the family and shares the prestigious client list that includes 1988 Tony winner Philip Bosco. Los Angeles liaison is Judy Schoen.

Agents
Alan Willig, Jacinthia Alexander, Bill Iaonne and Kiel Junius.
Client List
80
Clients
Philip Bosco, Max Wright, Joe Morton, Ving Rhames, Elaine Stritch, Pat Carroll, Keene Curtis, Kevin Gray, Karen Ziemba and others.
Notes

Silver, Kass & Massetti/East Ltd.

145 W 45th Street, #1204
btwn 6th & 7th Avenues
New York, NY 10030
212-391-4545

Monty Silver expected that his background as an actor,
stage manager, graduate school scenic designer and *gofer*
on Broadway would lead to a career in producing.
Actually, it did. His prestigious agency has not only
produced some important agents, but some prestigious
actors as well. Figuring to round out his show-biz
education with a six month stint at agenting, he accepted
Hilly Elkins' offer in 1957 and has been at it ever since.

He started his own office in 1961 and recently reorganized
the agency into a bi-coastal empire partnering with two of
his former agents, Robby Kass and Donna Massetti. Robby
and Donna work the west coast and Monty is still head-man
in New York. He is joined by colleagues Diane Busch
(whose background is casting) and nephew, Charles Silver.

One of the most successful and respected agents in the
business, Monty represents prestigious clients like Sylvia
Sidney, Celeste Holm and others as signed clients and free-
lances with 30 to 40 other actors whose careers he believes
in. His favorite client is one who continues to perfect his
craft. Monty feels this kind of client is always in the
mainstream because of constant study.

Agents
Monty Silver, Charles Silver and Dianne Busch.
Client List
125
Clients
James McDaniel, Paul Guilfoyle, Sylvia Sidney, Celeste Holm and others.
Notes

Susan Smith & Associates

192 Lexington Avenue, #1204
btwn 31st & 32nd Streets
New York, NY 10016
212-545-0500

The New York office of Susan Smith & Associates is now
headed by Joni Deakins. Susan Smith built her office in the
early 1970s and now divides her time mostly between Los
Angeles and London. Since Marcia McManus left the
agency, no one there will return my calls, so I have no first
hand information.

Agents
Joni Deakins.
Client List
70
Clients
Brian Dennehy, Greta Scacchi, Richard Masur, David
Paymer, Miranda Richardson and others.
Notes

The Starkman Agency

1501 Broadway, #301
btwn 43rd & 44th Streets
New York, NY 10036
212-921-9191

Do you know what I like about Marvin Starkman?
Everything. Marvin strikes me as the man you would want
to talk to when life is dark — or light, for that matter.
Originally a producer of films and television commercials,
Marvin (whose college major was directing) was surprised
when a job agenting for Monty Silver in the early 70s
presented a career that he absolutely loved. The one-to-one
relationships with actors and casting directors really
appealed to him. He opened his own office in 1977 after
five and a half years with Monty and has been representing
his clients with care and dedication ever since.

Career development is Marvin's strong point, so he prefers
working with signed clients. Recently he has taken on
strong literary clients Erik Jendresen, Victoria R. Herrick
and Richard Andrew Gaetta. Marvin's quotes elsewhere in
the book will give you more of an idea why I think Marvin
is so special.

Agents
Marvin Starkman.
Client List
35-40
Clients
Elaine Prince, Arch Johnson, Eliza Ventura,
Keith Hamilton Cobb, South Miller and others.
Notes

Peter Strain & Associates, Inc.

1500 Broadway, #2001
btwn 43rd & 44th Streets
New York, NY 10036
212-391-0380

Peter Strain studied directing at St. John's University and
directing at Circle-in-the Square. Unsure of a specific
target, he did know that he wanted to be involved in the
theater. Peter says his credentials for his first agenting job
were enthusiasm and enthusiasm. It seems to have been a
prime ingredient since Peter's list includes impressive
clients like Joe Mantegna, Faith Prince and Lindsay Crouse.
Peter's journey has taken him from Fifi Oscard Associates
to Jacobson/Wilder to Bauman Hiller & Strain and on to
APA before he started Peter Strain & Associates in 1988.

Peter enjoys the challenge of finding work for someone who
is not *dead on*. Colleague David Shaul has been Peter's
colleague since Bauman/Hiller & Strain. Charles Bodner
(STE) completes the roster of impressive agents. Peter's
Los Angeles liaison is The Marion Rosenberg Office.

Agents
Peter Strain, David Shaul and Charles Bodner.
Client List
70
Clients
Lindsay Crouse, Joe Montegna, Faith Prince, Bruno Kirby,
Rene Auberjonois, Frank Langella and others.
Notes

Talent East

340-A E 58th Street
btwn 1st & 2nd Avenues
New York, NY 10022
212-838-7191

Bob Donaghey started Talent East in February of 1992 and
since then, the agency has taken on a life of its own. Bob
has had a fascinating career from the moment he *got off the
bus* from Michigan with a theater degree. His first jobs
were as a page with CBS (during the week) and as Ed
Sullivan's assistant (on the weekends). The Sullivan job
involved dealing with all the talent and their agents and
managers. While attending to the comforts of Frank Sinatra
and the like for Sullivan, he was promoted from page to
Program Coordinator on all the shows after Cronkite till 11
p.m. His job entailed screening shows and negotiating with
advertising agencies.

He worked at Grey Advertising and Benton & Bowles
before joining J. Michael Bloom as a bookkeeper. Because
Bob knew so many people in the advertising agencies, they
kept calling him for talent. It didn't take Michael long to
make Bob an agent. Zoli hired him away from Michael,
but when Zoli died, Bob went back to advertising work at
D'Arcy McManus. He opened The Lure International
Talent Group, Inc. with a friend, but because he wanted to
concentrate on theater, film and television instead of
models, he left that partnership and started Talent East.
Since Bob started with only a legit department, casting
directors were drawn to Bob because they knew he was
serious about having good clients. This dedication to
quality has resulted in the agency growing by leaps and

bounds. Today, Talent East also represents clients for entertainment (bands), commercials, print and has just recently established a literary department.

Bob started his agency as a one man office in borrowed office space. By April he had his own office space and three other agents. Because Talent East is still building, they work only with free-lance talent in all fields.

Agents
Bob Donaghey, Carole Davis, H. Shep Pamplin, Johnny Puma.
Client List
free-lance
Clients
free-lance
Notes

Talent Representatives, Inc.

20 E 53rd Street
just E of 5th Avenue
New York, NY 10022
212-752-1835

Partners Honey Raider and Steve Kaplan met in 1962 when they were both briefly and accidentally involved in real estate. Steve had a background in advertising and in their idle moments between sales, they discussed theater, film, and television, trying to find a way to enter the business.

In 1964 they applied for a franchise and opened Talent Representatives. Today Honey handles 17 signed theatrical clients and Steve is the head of the commercial department. Glen Barnard (Lancit Media) is their colleague. This office has credibility and respect. Robert Edmunds is their assistant.

Agents
Honey Raider, Steve Kaplan and Glen Barnard.
Client List
17 + free-lance
Clients
Donald May, Carla Borelli, Walt Willey, Linda Dano, David Forsyth, Judi Evans and others.
Notes

Theater Artists Agency

250 W 57th Street, #1527-10
at Broadway
New York, NY 10019
212-867-0303

Robert Salmaggi started in the business back in 1966 as an
actor and a musician. Because he had one of the more
interesting *survival* jobs, working with a film laboratory and
seeing dailies, he was exposed to a different side of the
business and met directors, producers and cameramen. He
was making good money ($300 weekly) when he decided to
enter William Morris University via the mailroom on a
journey to become an agent. He worked as a floater and
assisted all the major executives in legit and films dealing
with Jack Lemon, Angela Lansbury and the like. Realizing
that to move from secretary to agent at WMA would entail
waiting for someone to leave or die, Salmaggi moved to
APA and became a personal appearance agent booking rock
and roll. He worked at Associated Booking before deciding
to move to Los Angeles to work with Jack Rose in order to
experience the business form the California perspective. He
returned home to New York in 1990 and started Theater
Artists Agency where he handles both writers and actors.

Agents
Robert Salmaggi.
Client List
80 + free-lance
Clients
Ted Baum, Ernst Gaudier, Marilyn Wise and others.
Notes

Michael Thomas Agency, Inc.

305 Madison Avenue, # 4419
on 42nd Street
New York, NY 10185
212-867-0303

Michael Thomas is one of the most genteel agents in the business. He hails from Georgia and it shows in his charm and integrity. After acting for a while, Michael had his first agenting job with Fifi Oscard Associates in 1959. Nine years later, he opened his own office. Agent Rozanne Gates has returned to this office after a five year hiatus. Annette Shear assists both agents.

Agents
Michael Thomas and Rozanne Gates.
Client List
20 + free-lance
Clients
Lynn Thigpen, Howard Rollins and others.
Notes

Waters and Nicolosi

1501 Broadway, #1305
btwn 43rd & 44th Streets
New York, NY 10036
212-302-8787

Actor/employment representative Bob Waters found a way
to combine his day job and showbusiness by becoming an
agent. Today the name of the agency reflects Bob's
longtime relationship with colleague Jean Nicolosi.
Nicolosi began her agenting career with Bob and continues
to be one of his strongest assets.

Waters and Nicolosi recently moved into a new suite of
offices, but, other than that, it's pretty much business as
usual. Before he opened his office in 1969, Bob learned
the business working with Dick Miller. He has about 30
happy signed clients and also handles a limited amount of
free-lance talent. Waters and Nicolosi has liaison
relationships with Los Angeles agents like Century Artists,
CNA and Irv Schechter Company.

Agents
Bob Waters and Jeanne Nicolosi.
Client List
30
Clients
Check SAG listings or The Players Guide.
Notes

Ann Wright Representatives

136 E 56th Street, 2C
btwn 3rd & Lexington Avenues
New York, NY 10022
212-832-0110

Long a force on the commercial scene with a limited
theatrical list, Ann Wright has refocused her agency. No
longer representing on-camera talent of any kind, Ann now
concentrates on important voice over talent while husband,
Dan presides over an prominent list of literary clients.

Trained as an actress at prestigious Boston University, Ann
joined the casting pool for CBS when she moved to New
York. She assisted legendary agent, Milton Goldman, was
a casting agent at several advertising agencies and worked
for Charles Tranum and Bret Adams before opening her
own agency.

Agents
Ann Wright and Dan Wright.
Client List
free-lance
Clients
Voice over only.
Notes

Writers & Artists Agency

19 W 44th Street, #1000
just W of 5th Avenue
New York, NY 10036
212-391-1112

When Joan Scott started her own agency in the 60s, she named it The Joan Scott Agency and only represented actors. Today, the agency is one of the most distinguished and powerful of the independent agencies with offices on both coasts, and a name that reflects the importance of the literary branch of the agency. Writers and Artists is famous for its tasteful group of talented actors, writers directors, *and* agents.

Philip Carlson left Susan Smith & Associates to guide the theatrical clients. Ex-production stage manager, Karen Friedman joins Philip representing the likes of Laura San Giancomo and Danton Stone. The agency does no freelance work at all.

Agents
Philip Carlson and Karen Friedman.
Client List
160 (both coasts)
Clients
Laura San Giancomo, Danton Stone and others.
Notes

Zoli Management, Inc.

3 W 18th Street, 5th Floor
just W of 5th Avenue
New York, NY 10011-4610
212-242-7490

Zoli, an agency known for beautiful models, was
established in 1970 by Zoltan Redessy. When he died in
1980, he left the agency to former employees Barbara Lantz
(who headed the women's division) and Victoria Pribble
(who headed the men's division).

Ricki Reingold (William Schuller Agency) now heads up
the film and television department of Zoli. Retired from
agenting from many years, Ricki filled in at Zoli from time
to time and when a permanent job was offered, Ricki
became an integral part of the agency.

Zoli works with free-lance models, so if you are young and
beautiful, Zoli would be a good resource for you.

Agents
Ricki Reingold.
Client List
beautiful free-lance
Clients
same thing
Notes

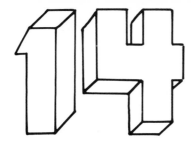

Index to Agents and Agencies

Kimble, John (82), (94), (134)
Kingman, Michael (49), (88)
Kintz, Robyne (190)
Kirk, Roseanne (211)
Kirsch, Karen (205)
Klein, Marty (172)
Kolker, Barry (228)
Kolker, Robert (161)
Koota, Raelle (200)
Kopelman, Charles (163)
Korman, Tom (172)
Krasny Office (9), (32), (35), (43), (80), (81)
Krasny, Gary (9), (32), (35), (43), (80), (81), (88), (100), (212), (213)
Kress, Victoria (187)
Kroll, Lucy (214), (215)
Kronick, Jane (216)
Kunsmen, Robert (183)
Lally Talent Agency (217)
Lally, Dale (217)
Landis, Scott (207)
Lantz Office (219)
Lantz, Robert (219), (220)
Larner, Lionel (11), (15), (23), (55), (90), (101), (189), (190), (222)
Latino, Victor (175)
Lauren, Ayn (216)
Laverly, Chip (201)
Leaverton, Gary (236)
Lebed, Holly (215)
Lee, Harris, Draper (228)
Leepson, Jonathan (189)
Leibmann, Sue (209)
Lerman, Peter (160)
Levy, Bruce (8), (25), (50), (68), (106), (108), (223)
Lewis, David (209)
Lieberman, Zoe (215)

Index to Everything Else

DARCY PALMER

Acting As A Business

Bryan O'Neil

SAMES & WAUNCK NO

CARSON NO

ABRAHMS GO

RICHARD ASTOR GO